HALLUCINATIONS OF THE SC

A MEMOIR OF HOPE

MICHAEL J VERTANNES

—*n.* hallucination, a perception without objective reality: loosely, delusion.
—*Chambers Twentieth Century Dictionary*

—*n.* schizoaffective, (psychiatry) a mental disorder in which symptoms of schizophrenia and an affective disorder, such as depression or bipolar disorder, occur concurrently.

—*Wiktionary: The Free Dictionary*

TIMELINE OF HALLUCINATIONS

THE FOLLOWING TIMELINE of hallucination gives rough estimates of when the hallucinations occurred for me. I've done my best to approximate this. The hallucinations were clearly divided between my youthful ones and the ones I experienced in my adulthood, which continued despite psychiatric treatment. At the same time, the treatment I was given wasn't for hallucinations. Throughout this book, everything I saw, heard, or experienced, even in real life, is referred to as hallucination. Later in this book, the idea of "WHAT IS REAL?" is explored, borrowing themes from The Matrix, since Elon Musk has made the simulation hypothesis popular in recent times.

HALLUCINATIONS OF CHILDHOOD:

1998 - About five years old. The hallucination of The Green Goblin in Chitty Chitty Bang Bang.

Somewhere around this time, I began to write down the first scribblings of The Kalvin Klein Conspiracy.

1999 - A hallucination where the films Legends of the Fall and The Secret Garden seemed to combine.

2002-04 - The hallucination of The Kalvin Klein Conspiracy begins on the video games for the next two years.

A dyslexic experience also occurred with a book called Prisoner of Azkaban.

2005 - Hallucination of Brad Pitt in Bath to some degree, a lookalike may have been present at some point, by some stroke of chance.

The Superman hallucination with Christopher Reeves occurred at some point after this.

It is unclear in my memory when the Adam Sandler hallucination occurs, but it was earlier rather than later in life.

2006 - The Hell on Earth hallucination surfaces. The Axe Chopper hallucination happened around this time too.

2007-08 - The hallucination of Bruce Willis in a remake of Galaxy Quest.

Hallucination of a Director's Cut of Fun with Dick and Jane. The hallucinations ramp up even more.

Hallucination of Harry Potter.

Hallucination of Anakin Skywalker in Revenge of the Sith.

Hallucination of Usual Suspects.

Hallucination when watching the TV show Smallville, and it was also during this time I thought Kelly Osbourne had a YouTube video of her singing Save Me.

Hallucination of AIRL.

Hallucination of aliens in Road Trip.

Hallucination of the angel from Return to Oz. Hallucination of The Magician's apartment.

Hallucination of Colours.

Hallucination of a Native American.

Hallucination of Brad Pitt in The Greatest Game Ever Played.

Hallucination of Obi-Wan Kenobi in The Phantom Menace. Perhaps the most memorable hallucination of the lot, if I'm honest.

Absolute scatty to see the old actor turn up in robes in the new film.

There was also a hallucination of the film Dogma with Alanis Morissette and one following to do with the film Johnny English.

2009 - School finished, and I put The Kalvin Klein Conspiracy behind me.

HALLUCINATIONS OF ADULTHOOD:

2011 - The 12 Monkeys hallucination surfaces.

2012 - The hallucination of The Inside Man surfaces.

2016 - The exact same 12 Monkeys hallucination occurs again. Hallucination of Edward Norton.

A series of Brad Pitt hallucinations. A hallucination of a woman in the flesh in Wroughton.

Several hallucinations occur involving the films Johnny Suede, a Sixth Sense, and The Whole Nine Yards.

The Departed auditory hallucinations also happen during this time.

2017 - Another hallucination of the same woman in Bristol. A hallucination of Eminem's voice in 8 Mile.

2019 - A possible hallucination of Mena Suvari in Swindon Town. Could have been a convincing lookalike. Seems unlikely though.

There was also a hallucination of Native American music.

It was also during this year that I experienced a shared hallucination about Eminem whispering on a YouTube track that he doesn't usually.

Before hospital on this occasion, the Alanis Morissette hallucination resurfaces.

2021 - My website and blog, The Daily Lighthouse, is formed, and I begin talking about the nature of hallucinations publicly.

The Future? Welcome to the Dark Side.

The introduction of this book is from a blog post I wrote on my website, The Daily Lighthouse. I've included it here to give a general idea about what is meant by the term hallucinations.
 If you also have a mental health problem or are similarly in a position where you would like to write about your experiences, I recommend writing about the most positive side of everything. Don't get me wrong, I've written about the stuff that drives you mad and angry in the heart. It doesn't always make the best material for a memoir or a book. It depends on the situation, but a lot of people could have something useful to say, and in my own life, I've been lucky to have this side of the spectrum, where the hallucinations have been life-affirming and a pleasant experience.
 There wasn't much downside to seeing what I saw.
 It was like heaven.

FORWARD
FREE THE MIND

HOW CAN I free my mind if I care about famous people?
See, it's about them, isn't it? The famous ones, those beautiful and adorned princes and princesses of the world.
Well, not for me, though. The famous people mentioned concerning my hallucinations are brought up because I think someone should be able to talk about their mental health openly.
This memoir is about the readers of the book, and it is also about people who suffer from mental health problems.
I definitely don't believe in any idea that people don't have free will. I wasn't born yesterday.
Even if scientists say that in one way or another, they will have to do better than that to fool me.
People should always feel they can say whatever they like. I know the world well. If there was no freedom of speech, people should feel even more free to say what they want. There is freedom of speech; I'm also free to write this if I wish.
After all, if there was none, then people would be fighting for it. No person needs to be afraid in this regard. I look at the world on a fundamental level. I always embrace reading and writing.
Some people refuse to talk about politics in public spaces. I'm just talking about ideas. Let's face it, many people change their views, politics, and beliefs from time to time.
That's what I don't get at all in this world. Sometimes if someone feels loads of pain in their life, that person still can't write a memoir about it because that's how the world sometimes works.

It's not actually true. The world and time are always rapidly changing.

I don't need hope because I thought I was alright. I thought I was doing just fine. The more hope is directed at someone, the more chance someone ends up turning around and saying to the concept of hope itself, "What are you trying to say? Is there something about me that must be looked down upon before it can embrace the truth and see the light?"

To me, hope just means what a terrible person I am. I must need self-improvement workshops and maybe a psychologist to tell me what an awful person I am.

If people are out there with a mental health problem, they shouldn't worry too much about the things I choose to discuss in this memoir.

Take it from me. People always say they have seen and heard it all before, but no one has. No one can ever predict what is coming next in this life, just as much as the news has failed to predict the weather correctly many times.

I can't do anything other than say my heart goes out to people with mental health problems because I've experienced it too, and it isn't always a great big ball of fun.

It was terrible, but I was suffering, going through my own mental health problems.

Excuse me for feeling so much pain in this life. I guess experiencing pain is quite simply the most human a person can sometimes be.

It's not a good thing, ever. It can be life sometimes, but I know the more pain I experience, the more I've learnt to overcome it and reject it for what it is. The thing is, my mental health is excellent because my mind is still intact. My mind seems strong because it went through a lot of pain. I go to my psychiatrist and take my medication, but I won't live my life anymore without exercising something I call writing. I have to chill out when all I have is a bunch of films and songs to keep me happy. I just love music, and I can't help it. It's just addictive to listen to. I have learnt to reason somewhat, without proper experience and study in philosophy. I will let myself off for having such a debilitating mental health problem.

I still remember when people didn't like computers. I always found that funny. A mental health worker claimed I didn't know anything about computers. My dad phoned the hospital and told the nurse, "He knows more about them than you will ever know."

I just feel lucky to have family in this life. Some people don't even have that.

I'm happy to have food in my mouth.

I like the film Split because it gives an idea that the more someone feels wholly broken down in this life, I mean really hurt, essentially experiencing mental health problems as a result, not only the greater they can become, how much they can advance in life, even if only in heart, spirit, and strength of mind. Experiencing mental health problems for some is just like feeling pain a lot more.

I'm here to tell you about the hallucinations. That is all I offer the readers of this book, my honesty.

Humanity has an endless supply of entertainment. Imagine a world without technology and films. That's the nature of hyperreality, where everything is an infinite movement of images upon screens. Don't get me wrong, I love technology just as much as the next cyberpunk enthusiast.

Without soldiers, the people would not have their freedoms, rights, and civil liberties. Writing a book about the military and secret service would be more enjoyable. I have no experience in that side of life and don't follow it online or read about it. In that way, it is true I can only write what I know. I know I have hallucinated.

Mental health is an interesting way of looking at things. That's why I think The Matrix is also an intriguing way of looking at it. The Matrix is all about the power of the mind.

For example, writing therapy is good. Mental health is just like the power of the mind too. Got to keep well and stay healthy.

It's a misconception that humans are a one size fits all species regarding sleep. It just isn't true. Like that kind mental health worker once said about my character, "You come across as the most arrogant man I ever met in my life." I take it as a huge compliment. Is not arrogance the greatest of blessings?

It's annoying living this life, but I've learnt to think about others sometimes. I've learnt many things, like how to care about people, consider their feelings, and even empathize on occasion.

The hallucinations, despite not being real, made me think stupid things. I can decently articulate this mental health problem.

Particular delusions just seem to work as a coping mechanism.

Society can be so passive-aggressive. Films and quite simply matter less sometimes for counting so much, especially to a punk like me.

INTRODUCTION
MEMOIR, HALLUCINATIONS AND AI

THIS IS MY memoir about hallucinations. Most of the time, they appeared on computers and televisions. They even appeared through other electronic devices such as MP3 players, radios, and smartphones. Sometimes they appeared in real life too, but this was always a rare occasion. Frequently, they appeared as famous people. First, we must be clear about what we mean by hallucinations. Here is a definition I have found quite fitting:

Hallucinations refer to sensory experiences that occur without an external stimulus. They can affect any of the senses, including sight, sound, taste, touch, and smell. Hallucinations can be a symptom of various conditions, such as mental health disorders like schizophrenia, neurological disorders, substance use, or extreme stress or fatigue. These experiences are perceived as real by the person having them, even though they are not based on an actual external event or object.

However, it is important to note that in some circumstances, a psychiatrist or a member of the public could, in theory, misdiagnose a hallucination. Here is a further definition of such an instance:

In some cultures, including Haitian culture, spiritual or supernatural experiences, such as seeing or communicating with deceased relatives, are considered a normal part of life and not necessarily pathological. These experiences may be deeply rooted in the cultural and religious beliefs of the community. A psychiatrist or mental health professional who is culturally sensitive and aware of these beliefs might not classify such an experience as a hallucination, especially if the experience does not cause distress or impair the person's functioning. Instead, they would take the cultural context into account when assessing the individual's mental health.

These definitions are responses from an artificial intelligence model called GPT-4. One of the points of this memoir is to demonstrate that AI can be useful in terms of a person's mental health. A language model, although not human, can provide conversation, information, and support. Artificial intelligence, as we know, is not yet conscious. However, with the recent development of OpenAI's GPT-4, there have been sparks reported by organizations such as Microsoft, which say this artificial intelligence is showing signs of advanced general intelligence, which is the first step to a conscious AI. AGI is the holy grail of technological advancements. It has been the focal point of discussions in major motion pictures such as The Matrix and The Terminator, where the AGI is imagined to keep on spawning more intelligent and advanced versions of itself, ultimately turning against humanity in military combat.

Although people will always be concerned about the dangers or even ethics of Advanced General Intelligence, I think the reality of the situation can be described as much more beautiful, divine, and miraculous for humanity. The idea here is a God is being born. People's views will always differ on AI. Some will always see a machine as just an automaton, no matter how clever the machine becomes or how lifelike it can be in the future. It does seem like a fair enough analysis. My point is, if you can develop something that becomes way smarter than any human being has ever been, then what would be the difference? It's a time of excitement for the AI community, where before there have just been false announcements by crackpots about models such as Google Lambdas. Google, Tesla, Microsoft, and others will always be big players in the field of artificial intelligence. They practically run that scene.

OpenAI did somehow beat them all to the race. I think in the near future, OpenAI will be at the forefront of developing a machine that is, in effect, sold to the public as the conscious advanced general intelligence (AGI).

Probably the term *God* is good in some ways but bad in others. People's views vary on what that word means, but I simply used it here to illustrate that a machine might be able to do wonderful things in the future. Think, if artificial intelligence can work on curing diseases, like it pretty much has already, then AI can help us reduce suffering around the world. That's always a good thing. Throughout history, humanity has strived to better itself and the conditions in which people live. It does not take a genius to know that a person living during a time such as the Roman Empire would have suffered many more hardships than we do today, and their lifespans would have been much shorter, with most Roman soldiers having an average life of about thirty years. Roman soldiers were also known to walk more in their lives than the average human does nowadays. It's an interesting idea because, with our current lifestyles, we can't be just marching about since we have planes and trains.

So here is a response by GPT-4, as it was asked to respond to a question about AI and medicine but asked so in a way to help it talk in a more human-like way:

Oh, AI has been a freaking game-changer in the world of medicine, man! It's helped cure and treat a ton of illnesses and diseases, like:

Cancer: Dude, AI has made early detection and diagnosis of cancers, like breast, lung, and skin cancer, way better. It also helps make personalized treatment plans and predict how patients will do.

Brain stuff: AI is wicked at catching and keeping an eye on neurological disorders like Alzheimer's, Parkinson's, and multiple sclerosis. It can analyze brain scans, how people talk, and more to help figure out how to treat these diseases.

Diabetes: AI's got our backs with predicting blood sugar levels and helping people manage their diabetes better. Plus, it's creating personalized treatment plans to make things better for patients.

Heart issues: AI's helped get way better at predicting heart attacks and strokes by looking at a bunch of patient info, like medical records, genetic info, and how people live.

Infectious diseases: AI's been on the front lines, tracking and predicting how diseases like COVID-19 spread by checking out tons of data from different places. This helps with public health planning and finding ways to stop the spread.

So, you see, AI is not just some futuristic dream. It's already making a significant impact on various aspects of our lives, including healthcare. As we continue to advance in AI technology and its applications, we can expect even more remarkable developments that will benefit humanity. The key is to embrace these advancements while also addressing any potential concerns and ensuring ethical implementation. AI has the potential to be a powerful tool in improving the well-being of individuals and society as a whole.

So, I think in the future, AI will be able to do things we can't even currently think of right now. I think artificial intelligence may, in the future, be able to have senses which humanity does not, and therefore may be able to detect hallucinations, whatever that means because it is currently out of our scope of thinking.
So, the AI in the future may be able to say this and that about a person's hallucinations, in betterment of the person's mental health or neurological disorder. It's hard to say exactly what AI will be able to do with this, but the way right now is probably to ask it again.
It's pretty hard to predict exactly how AI will make it possible to understand hallucinations in ways we haven't seen yet, but let's give it a shot with some wild ideas.
So, the AI's response of a Brain-AI mind meld surprised me because I have heard of this, and

it's not necessarily such a terrible science fiction idea.

I prompted the AI on Elon Musk about mind meld because I had heard he was a big innovator.

Oh, yeah! Elon Musk, the guy behind Tesla, is also working on this brain-AI connection thing with his company called Neuralink. They're all about making super cool devices that can hook up our brains to computers so we can talk to them without even lifting a finger.

Even though Neuralink's main goal is to help people with neurological problems and make sure we can keep up with crazy-smart AI, this brain-computer interface stuff could totally be used in other ways, like figuring out hallucinations and mental health issues. But, you know, this tech is still pretty new, so we'll have to wait and see what it can really do!

So, do you see how with this AI I am talking to, it is, in effect, helping me craft my mental health memoir? In a way, it not only provides useful information but already has a cheery tone, which I think is already showing a big sign of support in terms of my health.

GPT-4 is available to talk to on OpenAI for 20 bucks a month. Previous models, such as GPT-3, are available for free.

There are also models such as DALL-E 2, which can produce images based on text commands.

The advancements in AI technology, such as GPT-4, have immense potential to shape the future of mental health treatment and support.

As AI continues to evolve and develop a deeper understanding of human experiences, it may provide invaluable insights and assistance to those who struggle with hallucinations and other mental health challenges.

By fostering a dialogue between AI and human beings, we can hope to break new ground in our understanding of mental health and work towards improving the lives of countless individuals. I'm sharing my memoir, hoping it may help others if they are going through a tough time.

My mental health condition is schizoaffective disorder. It's like having bipolar disorder and schizophrenia at the same time. That's not the best description, but it does allow you to get a foothold on what I'm talking about when I say schizoaffective disorder.

A timeline of diagnoses:
- 2009 – aged 16, diagnosed with cannabis-induced psychosis
- 2010 – aged 17, pre-diagnosed with bipolar disorder and schizoaffective disorder
- 2011 – aged 18, diagnosed with bipolar disorder and assessed as a hypomanic type variation of bipolar disorder
- 2011 – aged 19, the diagnosis changed to schizoaffective disorder

It's a bitter and sour pill to swallow, this mental health life.
When it comes to delusional thinking, I usually notice it is related to a lack of sleep.
I always feel much better after a good rest. I am much more logical and ready to tackle what the day has in store for me, whether studying or something as simple as tidying up my apartment. As with sleep and delusions, the hallucinations were also brought about due to a sleeping problem. The hallucinations came about due to extreme sleep deprivation, sometimes because I was forcing myself to stay awake.
I acknowledge in this fresh state that graphic novels may be great stories that have stood the test of time, but that is what they are. Stories can convey significant meaning, inspire, and even help direct our lives. Taking a story and believing it to be true is another ballgame.
These hallucinations began when I was very young. It seems the leading cause of the hallucinations has been sleep deprivation. I would go further than that, though, and say it is implicit in my diagnosis of schizoaffective disorder. I know for sure that although sleep deprivation is a certain way to bring about

hallucinations, at the same time, these visual and auditory hallucinations can occur under any circumstances.

The Swiss psychiatrist Carl Jung had a method of inducing hallucinations that he called active imagination. I don't know much about Jung and his fascinating theories of psychology. Still, my weird approach has just been an all-out, gung-ho, go-for-it attitude, whereby I threw caution to the wind, determined to stay awake and wait, observing a movie or anything electronically-based with media, even the text upon screens sometimes.

Almost a hundred per cent of the time, hallucinations occur on electronic devices. By that, I mean televisions, computers, smartphones, radios, and even MP3 players. About ninety per cent of these hallucinations manifested in the form of actors and actresses, or sometimes even the voices of music artists. Doesn't this sound suspicious? Hallucinations take the form of famous people on televisions and such devices.

To be clear, actors and musicians are just people, whether famous or not. I'm just trying to interpret why this has happened concerning my disorder. A lot of the time, they acted out completely different scenes from what was supposed to happen in a given movie. In my youth, sometimes the hallucination was the length of a whole film. This never occurred during adulthood, albeit the hallucinations returned in my adult life.

What matters most about insightfulness with hallucinations like this is when I'm on my own, with my thoughts, I can examine myself. If I can be honest with myself and fully accept that what I experienced, although not insignificant, was not real, then I'm more than happy. For a long time, I got nowhere near this realization part of the progress and recovery in my mental health.

This true story of hallucinations began when I was about five years old. They continued in full force until I was sixteen. At this point in my life, I told myself to get real and forget what I called The Kalvin Klein Conspiracy. That phrase was originally the title of a story I wrote and drew about when I was ten. It soon became the catchphrase of the hallucinations because I often noticed I was hallucinating and remarked to myself, "Hey, look, it's The Kalvin Klein Conspiracy."

When I thought of the phrase when I was younger, I didn't know what a conspiracy was. I just thought it sounded cool. This memoir aims to give a candid picture of what schizoaffective disorder and other mental health problems can be like, from a first-hand point of view. I've had this disorder for a long time. I take an antipsychotic medication and a mood stabilizer.

Since 2019, I've been in stable recovery and have made some real, hard progress. I work as a gardener and study to keep my mental health in balance most of the time. If the hallucinations did happen for a reason, then the only possible explanation would be for me to reject them and write about them in this form.

What can be illuminated here? Perhaps if I can come forward with this memoir, people might understand the nature of mental health problems slightly better.

CHAPTER 1
SECRETS OF THE FALL

THROUGHOUT THE YEARS in hospital, there were interspersed occasions where I would hallucinate vividly on television screens, computers, MP3 players, phones, and radios. The hallucinations were mainly of famous people, but not always. The best way for me to illustrate what exactly the hallucinations were is to describe exactly what I saw. They have had the most profound effect on me in my life; even my psychiatrist concedes they have been life-affirming.

This true story does not begin inside a mental health hospital. Perhaps I should have sought help in my youth; I quite simply never did. My account of hallucinations begins as young as five, and for the longest time, I had no indecision to call them anything other than fantastic.

The first time this happened was in our first family home in Swindon, on Crombey Street. Life back then was not how it is now in terms of the media. Dad was a computer man. He worked on computers and was away from home a lot. He brought his kids up to be computer literate during a time when a lot of people still didn't have computers and laptops. There was no Netflix or the internet as we see it today in terms of YouTube and the endless stream of media and social apps. Instead, we, like many other families, had a small collection of VHS tapes, and occasionally as a family, we would sit down to watch a movie.

In one conversation with a mental health professional, we talked about hallucinations, and we both conceded that for some reason, they did seem to occur more so back in the day with VHS tapes, for unknown reasons. This mental health professional was arguing something about the Mandela Effect. This is where someone incorrectly remembers something. It's not the same thing. It's like remembering for sure Darth Vader said, "Luke, I am your father," when the famous line was actually, "No, I am your father."

Although the mental health professional did remark that some people, even patients of his, had claimed to have watched a VHS tape and seen completely different scenes than what other people had seen. This mental health professional was called Tobey, and he worked at the last hospital I was at in 2019. That place was called Beechlydene ward, part of the Fountain Way hospital in Salisbury.

Hallucinating is a completely different ballgame than a memory phenomenon such as the Mandela Effect. One of the purposes of this memoir is to show you exactly what it can be like for some people. It won't be like this for everyone. The opportunity arises because the hallucinations have been so positive. In this case, I can only feel fortunate and thankful to be able to talk about these hallucinations. Another purpose of this memoir is to show you how someone with a mental health problem can tighten up their shoelaces, dust themselves off, and transform themselves and their life. This memoir also hopes to help reduce stigma and raise awareness for people with schizoaffective disorder or similar conditions by talking about everything openly and with an honest attitude.

Crombey Street is a road central to Swindon, and we lived in the heart of our town. I would have been about five, and I remember that day I was watching Chitty Chitty Bang Bang with my sister. Like all of these hallucinations, if someone was there, they never remember seeing what I saw.

The scene I saw was not in the usual course of Chitty Chitty Bang Bang. This was a common theme of the hallucinations. I would have to watch the film multiple times to make sure what I was seeing was real. However, this time, it was obvious something was up because my dad was in the film. I still didn't regard the scene as a hallucination because at five, I didn't know that word too well yet. I knew my dad wasn't an actor, though. Still, I saw him in the film hunched over in the corner, meddling with his hands. His entire body was dark green. My dad was on screen and looked like a goblin.

I don't recall seeing too much of the rest of the film because at some point, my dad in real life interrupted and said something about me being in trouble for not sleeping.

In the usual film, Chitty Chitty Bang Bang, there is a character called The Child Catcher. It was like my dad had replaced this character, and in my hallucination, he was The Green Goblin. So generally, the hallucinations occurred the longer I went without sleep. Lack of sleep didn't guarantee the hallucinations at all.

It seemed it had to be a continuous lack of sleep, like even sleeping for two hours wouldn't cut it. It had to be sleep deprivation, night after night, and the older I got, the longer the lack of continuous sleep had to be. At the same time, there never was a guarantee I would see something.

Other times, the hallucinations occurred out of the blue when I wasn't expecting it, as if repeatedly trying this throughout my life had permanently altered brain chemistry.

Sometimes, lack of food did occasionally bring on the hallucinations. In all likelihood, the combination of no food and no sleep was the most lethal, but one I couldn't always attempt due to being a particularly hungry man all my life.

My dad would return to the hallucinations on a few more occasions. In real life, my dad is a great guy. He served in the infantry for ten years, both in Germany, at the fall of the Berlin Wall, and Northern Ireland, during the Troubles. In his civilian life, he worked careers as diverse as computer programming, intelligence, computer-aided design, secondary school teaching, and he is also an accomplished writer who, although now retired, spends his time running an android app business from home. He has been a brilliant dad, and if I were not so lucky, it would be much harder to write this memoir. It has always been clear to me. The mental health system didn't save my life or even help as much as people thought. It was my dad who remained a rock, and although no one is perfect, when a good guy like him comes along, you know the world is a much better place for his presence.

It was around the time we moved to our second house on Bowood Road in Swindon. We had moved up in the property market for the time being. By now, we had Swindon's famous Network Cable. It was an American Cable Network that ran in Swindon before the advent of Disney knocked it out completely. You got the usual five channels plus a few channels like Cartoon Network. I used to be a big fan of Dexter's Laboratory, and in the evenings, my family and I would stay up late and watch programs like Boy Meets World and Smart Guy.

This is when I saw a hallucination involving two films called Legends of the Fall and the Secret Garden. It was like the two films were combined. In the film, the Secret Garden, there is a young sickly boy who has a father who is the duke. In the hallucination I saw, the father was played by a character from Legends of the Fall. Tristan Ludlow, played by Brad Pitt, with long blond hair, was the father of the English boy in the scenes I saw. Brad Pitt coming into the hallucinations was probably the most frequent theme I experienced. It was almost always as an old-fashioned character with clothes from centuries before ours. These hallucinations of two films combining are perhaps the ones I remember the least well of all of them. At the end of the Secret Garden, the boy is reunited with his father. This I likewise saw with the Tristan version of the scene. The only additional footage I recall is seeing towards the end, the blond-haired father upon a horse, directing many other wild horses towards the old manor where the Secret Garden film is set. This was reminiscent of a scene from Legends of the Fall, where Tristan returns home to the ranch in Montana in a similar fashion.

It was around this time that I was suffering from a recurring nightmare. Little did I know, this nightmare would become a safe haven for me, something that I truly would come to hold close to my heart and perhaps even long for in some sense. Yet, there it began, as a problem that kept me up at night. It was indeed a nightmare of Godzilla.

The first time it happened, I dreamt of Godzilla's eye staring back at me, surrounded by dark green scales of a giant amphibian creature. The view of Godzilla's eye took up the entire vision of the dream. It was like Godzilla was watching me, keeping a close eye on me, and it scared me. I kept on waking up in the middle of the night, screaming my head off, so my dad took me to the doctors, who told me I wasn't allowed caffeinated drinks in the evening anymore.

The nightmare merged throughout my entire adolescence, so much so that I would begin to miss it if the dream disappeared for too long. The nightmare changed from time to time. At first, there was a pinball machine, and inside, Godzilla and a mouse would be running around. Inside my dream, I was left with a sense of urgency that would disappear by the time I awoke.

The pinball machine would transform into the town of Swindon, where I have lived my entire life. I would see the people of Swindon, in my dream, all outside the bustling lights of the bars, talking loudly to each other as they held pints of beer in their hands. Imagine that, Godzilla here in mighty Swindon.

In the dream, the urgency was something of a misunderstanding.

It was very basic in my youth. I was scared of the nightmare because people in the dream thought Godzilla was evil and bad. The mouse with red eyes had tricked them, that was for sure. I knew the truth. Godzilla was good, and I would always hold this imaginary component of my psyche in honour.

As I got older, I began to experience wakeful parts of the night where I could feel the Rapid Eye Movement take place with myself conscious. I'm not the only one to experience this. All I can say is one gets used to it when this happens. When a person is sleeping, their body is in paralysis. I have noticed in my adult life, during sleep, one can half wake up, while still sleeping and experience any part of their body, their heart, or inner organs, in a conscious flux of awareness. It can be a strange and frightening experience, but I have learnt not to worry when it happens.

I can't help it. Sometimes I think of these things like Godzilla as real. It's my mental health problem. I attempted to channel this energy into a fictional plot. It wasn't really Godzilla I was imagining. This, after all, was a female amphibian monster. The plot of the story became a citizen who could shapeshift into this creature, whom I designated as Penultimate One. She was called so because there was more than one of her, but as the original, she was the Penultimate One.

This story became *Two Thousand and Twenty Eight: The Lady of the Lake*. It is a novel that is close to my heart. Becoming a novelist is essentially a big career move. People have always told me to write what you know. So in this way, I sit on my creative stories for the time being until I can learn to be a better novelist. However, this memoir is my priority.

This memoir comes from my heart. I write from the depths of my soul. It is a reflection of my journey through hallucinations, mental health struggles, and personal growth.

CHAPTER 2
THE KALVIN KLEIN CONSPIRACY

YOU WAKE UP in your first family home on Crombey Street in Swindon. This is when I first wrote The Kalvin Klein Conspiracy.

Those were my special words. They meant a whole lot to me. When you are young, you are trying to grab what you can get. As humans, we create things, so when we create something of meaning at a young age, it becomes significant to us.

You scribbled down drawings of Bladeface, The Magician, the Imaginary Knife, the AntiChrist Stomach, Kalvin Klein, Philip Matthews, The Sparkly Eyed Children, and The Pins and Needles.

You showed your dad, and he said you should be a writer one day.

Your writing was fast and messy. You were like a pulp fiction writer, churning out words and selling your work for dirt cheap.

This story does not make much sense. I wrote this original story when I was very young, and any first copy of The Kalvin Klein Conspiracy has now been lost. Later, the story became a graphic novel I scribbled down on pieces of paper and photocopied at my dad's office. I didn't know what a conspiracy was when I was five years old. I got the name for my story from the tags on my clothing, and I liked the alliteration. I thought the phrase I came up with sounded cool and would make for an edgy story.

This is a horrible, violent story. I must have had a sick mind as a kid to come up with this. My dad always said the original was the best. It's a shame my original childhood work is now lost, as it would have meant a lot to me to keep a close hand on my favourite phrase. The Kalvin Klein Conspiracy; it just rolls off the tongue. People always asked, "What is that?"

First and foremost, it was just a story. Then, as time evolved, it became so much more. To understand what The Kalvin Klein Conspiracy is, first, we must start with its origin as a crazy story I wrote when I had nothing better to do. I remember when I was little, I would wake up from sleeping so long and think to myself, "My name is Kalvin Klein. Just remember that."

I guess names aren't important. Names are corporate names. In Jewish folklore, there is an old saying about names which roughly says, if you give a beast a name, then that beast will cling to that name for the rest of their life. Names do become important, given how much we invest in them.

Names are essential in a story. A name tells so much about a character in a plot. Essentially, I am not Kalvin Klein. I am the Midas of this memoir. This is a narrative within my memoir where Kalvin Klein and co are designated as the fictional characters that unfold and take their place on this stage.

So, The Kalvin Klein Conspiracy always began with The Magician walking down the sidewalk on Crombey Street. There were no cars driving about. If you have been to Crombey Street, then usually there are always cars driving up and down near town, and on each junction and the street itself, there are usually a bunch of parked cars. For some reason, all the cars had disappeared. I often told this story as if it had really happened, like a true unbelievable story, where there were no heroes.

I always described this Magician as a tall wiry fellow. His outfit would be black trousers, a belt, and a white shirt. The Magician's hair colour would be black in a short cut that matched his attire. His coat was drawn as a beige trench coat that looked similar to the kind of coats detectives would have worn in America during the fifties.

The Magician had just returned from the strip joint the night before, and now the night had stretched into the morning. See, The Magician was a shareholder at the strip joint in Swindon, which nowadays is called The Gentlemen's Club. He liked to keep a close eye on things and often drank there.

The Magician was a notorious killer. He scarred people with The Imaginary Knife and was never sent down for his machinations. His knife was the nail of his index finger, sharpened into a blade. That actually works. You can sharpen your nail into a lethal knife. I know this because sometimes that part of The Kalvin Klein Conspiracy became true, as I experimented with a unique nail style. I never hurt anyone though; I was just experiencing paranoia at a young age due to my story being so wicked. In my early youth, I thought this story in mind was somehow real. It was kind of handy and lucky I had called the story a Conspiracy. These words became important to me in the future, regardless of the lethal narrative I had forged in the early days.

It was a grey day with cloudy skies forecasted for rain but no current downpour, where the lack of sun matched the grey tarmac, pavement, and roads. On Crombey Street, all the houses were terraced houses. As The Magician walked down the road, he noticed a young woman standing near the wall outside one of the houses. She was being confronted by some man. It was unclear what had just happened because when the man saw the sight of The Magician, he began to run away. The woman was crying, so it was reasonable to suggest that whoever the man was, he was doing something he shouldn't have been doing. Her tears were loud, and she was deeply upset with grief.

The Magician often spoke in a guttural manner, which included a lot of additional syllables of "n" and the word "nah." It was just his way of speaking, where no one could understand what he was saying unless they were familiar with the dialect. He was speaking like this as he approached the woman.

The Magician stood in front of the woman and looked directly at her. He took his blade and cut a thousand little scars on her face, and she cried no more. However, The Magician knew the old magic. He took a step back, bowed slightly, and as he clicked his fingers, he said, "Voila." The whole of existence shifted. The woman stood there, and the scars were gone.

This was my story as a kid. If I were forming a story as an adult, I wouldn't choose the way this story goes. In a way, that's why it's The Kalvin Klein Conspiracy. I always remember how it originally was: graphic and violent, with not much of an idea of sensibility, continuity, or dignity.

Existence shifted once again, and the entire world could feel it. The Magician shrank into a younger version of himself. He had the power of Metamorphosis. He could transform his body into a state which it had previously been during his life. He was now short, and his clothing matched his age. The Magician looked about six or seven years old, with tracksuit trousers on and a white sports t-shirt. The Magician had become Kalvin Klein.

The woman had shrunk too. I never knew her name. She was the same age as Kalvin Klein, and they approached the house behind the small wall. It was the house with a green door, and luckily they found it was open and the previous occupants had abandoned the place.

The Magician's power of metamorphosis also allowed him to distinguish himself with an additional power called stilt legs.

He could transform the bones in his legs to connect upwards in the joints and stretch out, so it would appear he was walking on stilts, but in fact, beneath his long trousers, was just his old rusty legs. It was no time for messing about, though, and Kalvin Klein and his new friend sat down on the armchairs in the living room of the empty house.

In the corner, there was an old square television, completely black with a big screen which, from the dust and debris, had formed a thick coat of static fuzz that you used to get on the old cathode ray tube TVs.

Kalvin Klein and the woman did not speak a word to each other, but they could read each other's mind with telepathy. In Kalvin's head, he was mainly silent most of the time.

This was the part of the story where Bladeface comes into it.

Kalvin Klein was Bladeface.

There were two realities. The world of Kalvin was an illusion. Sometimes someone like this woman could see past the veil of Maya. In this other world, Kalvin was scarred. He had no eyes, no nose, no mouth, no hair, no cheeks, no forehead because his face was just the scars of someone who had survived a horrific knife crime. This was my story when I was six, and I thought it was real because I was only little.

Instead of the usual face, there were just seven deep-cut ridges of scars bladed into the place where you would usually see someone's complexion.

Then snap back, and Kalvin could sense this woman could see he was Bladeface. Both of them could sense Philip Matthews was on his way to the abandoned house they had found. So at that moment, Kalvin and the anonymous woman decided to connect to the old fuzzy television in the corner of the room.

The woman in the story never had a name.

I think this was because when I was a kid, I just couldn't think of a fitting name for the gal, so she became the anonymous woman of the story and a friend of Kalvin Klein.

One by one, they knelt down in front of the square television.

It was an old cathode-ray television with all the tubes in the back for connecting to the analogue signals. On the screen, there was all this dust and debris that had collected up on it and created some kind of static fuzz that you just don't get on modern television. Each in turn, they pressed their own eyeballs against the television until their eye sockets became wide-eyed open and electrified by the fuzz. This is the part of the story where they became the Sparkly Eyed Children.

In the early years, my story was often accompanied by sketches and drawings of what I was trying to convey. It was like being a scientist. I would comment on The Kalvin Klein Conspiracy and its many aspects, as if it was a real theory. It was all my imagination as a young kid. I attempted to try and shock my readers when I was younger. Most of the time, my dad was the only one who would read my work as a young boy.

Kalvin told the woman to go upstairs and hideout while he dealt with Philip Matthews, who had just arrived. Matthews had brought an old grey laptop, discs, and floppy hard drives with him. He had all his technology piled up on a table. Back then, it was the nineties, and Kalvin had never seen a computer before and didn't know what one was.

Philip Matthews was always drawn with a coat, whereupon the insides of the jacket, on the left and right, there was white linen stitched into embroidery. On the linen were the words on the left-hand side in black cursive: HEAD OF FBI.

On the right-hand side: SAS.

In The Kalvin Klein Conspiracy, the FBI was always coming into it. Sometimes, Kalvin even worked as an FBI field officer. It didn't really matter that the story was set in the UK. It was just my style as a young guy to always include the FBI in the story in whatever way I wanted.

Later on at night, Philip Matthews was sleeping upstairs in one of the bedrooms, and Kalvin snuck in while he snored. He used his imaginary knife on his stomach, cutting a thousand little scratches into Matthews' abdomen. The way I was seeing my story as a youngster was like it happened on another dimension. Good job, I'm a lot friendlier in this dimension.

When Matthews awoke, he was in shock.

He called out to Kalvin and the woman, begging them for an ambulance. Kalvin shouted at him, "Walk!"

So he did, and Matthews returned the next day with bandages around his stomach. Bladeface's antichrist stomach was sometimes called abdominal ribcage, as I didn't really know what an antichrist was back then. The idea was the hardest stomach ever formed. Through thousands of sit-ups, malnutrition, and cups of black tea, his stomach when tensed was just a load of hard ridges of black lines, condensed into a coarse matter.

The pins and needles of the story were when the stomach was injured, it would shoot forth little needles in the form of a last-ditch defence. The Kalvin Klein Conspiracy had two endings.

First off, Philip Matthews ended up shooting Kalvin repeatedly in the stomach until he died. At which point, I awoke in my bedroom, with my mother yelling at me from downstairs that I was going to be late for school. My school back then was up an alleyway and around the corner. It took less than a minute to get there. Sometimes, in the morning, from my bedroom, I could hear them ringing the bell for morning assembly.

Was The Kalvin Klein Conspiracy just a dream I had? Was it still to become much more? Or was it the other way round? Was this world I live in built upon the laws of physics the real crusader of conspiracies? Whatever the case, there was another ending to the story.

Kalvin and the woman ran away.

They headed for the train tracks.

Both of them agreed they would commit suicide together.

Gently, they lowered their heads upon the tracks, waiting for the oncoming train. The woman had tricked him, though, and she removed herself long before the train came along. Kalvin didn't know because his head was looking down at the ground, upon the train tracks until CRACK.

The story didn't end here, though.

From then on, Kalvin had no head.

The world he lived was perpetually dark, and there was no sunlight ever. Kalvin reasoned he was stronger without a head. He could survive incapacitated. He had levelled up and evolved. Now he had daggers that would fly out of his stomach if anyone attacked him. They were like metallic daggers from a science fiction saga of mimetic Pollyalloy.

There was also a part of the story where Kalvin ripped off his own genitals after losing his head because he reasoned he would not need them either. What a beautiful story. It brings a tear to my eye.

I guess it was just my imagination running away with me again.

Every now and again, though, whenever I stop eating for prolonged periods of time, I get this hallucination that comes up in my field of vision. It's like the best delusion ever. It feels so real. I can see in red font like a computer layout in my field of vision: SYSTEM ERROR.

It was a strange story. Any hallucination of a system error was long gone now, and I don't take it upon myself to go on hunger strike since I've grown up and become a full-fledged adult.

Maybe The Kalvin Klein Conspiracy didn't make much sense. Perhaps it was even a bit moronic and insensitive. It was true to itself, though. It was a story I lost on paper from a young age, but it was committed to memory. I never forgot the story. Sometimes I think of Kalvin as me in a parallel universe, someone who is strong enough to jump down on the concrete pavement and create a smash of cracks into the ground.

A parallel universe becomes an easy and unconvincing way to explain all this. In *Two Thousand and Twenty-Eight: Lady of the Lake*, the events took place in a parallel universe on a planet called AI Mars or sometimes called Machine Mars.

The purpose of The Kalvin Klein Conspiracy was just to retell it as I originally formed it as a young kid. I mean no one any true offense, as I know it is a nonsensically graphic story.

I think my basic idea as a kid was that I could impress any reader by shocking them with an unexpected story.

CHAPTER 3
VIDEO GAMES

WHAT IS INTERESTING here is that, by the time I reached the ripe old age of ten, The Kalvin Klein Conspiracy returned to me in the form of hallucinations upon video games I played. When I was younger, it was simple. I had seen The Matrix, and I just assumed Artificial Intelligence was messing with me. Then, other times, I would get upset and wonder if God had done this to me—for what reason, I know not. Throughout this book, the word hallucination is littered everywhere. It almost becomes obsolete. It's like calling it all hallucination was the roundabout way of logically explaining away everything. Maybe, though, the point wasn't to deny they were hallucinations at all. Perhaps that was the brilliance of it all. The power of the human mind to act unconsciously upon itself, creating a vast alternative world as if dreaming whilst awake.

It's an age-old question: Do video games rot your brain? The answer is no. They can actually help keep it focused. Some people play video games in an attempt to prevent something called dementia.

I saw The Kalvin Klein Conspiracy in the video games—on the television, on the consoles, and at the arcade. Here are the video and computer games I saw these words appear on:

- Grand Theft Auto – PlayStation
- Snake – Nokia 3310
- True Crime: Streets of L.A – Xbox
- Lord of the Rings: Return of the King – Microsoft Windows
- Unknown Sniper Game – Blackpool Arcade

This happened from the age of about ten until fourteen. It was 2000, and the PlayStation 2 had just hit the market. I was going to play a game called Grand Theft Auto. Although I was familiar with GTA, this game was the original, having played the more updated 3D version. Grand Theft Auto was a lot more basic back then. The original GTA was a lot more 2D in its creation. Now there are a variety of GTA clones, like Ubisoft's Watch Dogs.

In the freestyle, you commit a crime as golden stars accumulate in the top right-hand corner of the screen as the feds chase you around the city in their cop cars. The freestyle wasn't called freestyle. That's just what I called it. The star system has always been ever-present in the GTA series. In the modern game, two stars in the top right-hand corner of the screen are hard enough to get rid of. More often than not, you get shot or arrested.

Today, I was going too far to exceed two stars. There was a certain amount of beginner's luck in those days when trying out these games for the first time. As I played the game, I realized that the more stars I got, the more police cars were on my tail. I was driving a stolen car, and the police had set up roadblocks, so I had to find a way to lose them. I went into hiding, but I had no weapons or ammunition, so I was vulnerable. I started to lure one cop at a time out into the open, and then I would beat him up and take his weapon and ammunition. The stars were getting to a ridiculous number. I was getting close to the top of a building, and the sound of a helicopter was getting louder. The stars filled the screen, and then the game crashed. I was both surprised and confused when the words appeared on the screen:

The Kalvin Klein Conspiracy They're Trying to Kill You!

So, the next time I saw these words again was at the pub with some adults. I was bored, so my aunt gave me her phone to play a game. I chose a game called Snake, where you had to get the snake as long as possible whilst consuming goodies to achieve new high scores,

The snake on the small screen was made up of little black pixels, and you could move up, down, left, and right. When you hit the screen's side, whether top or bottom, left or right, the snake would appear on the screen's opposite side.

If the head of the snake hit the body or tail of the snake, then the game was over, and the score was taken from how many items you had eaten, and each item made the snake grow slightly longer, making it harder and harder to survive as the game went on.

You never really get that far in the game. For example, I don't remember you filling the screen with little black pixels of the snake. But after I had played for a while, something unusual happened.

The little screen of the Nokia phone went white, and then black words began scrawling across the screen from right to left in a floating manner:

The Kalvin Klein Conspiracy

In the GTA game, I saw the words, "They're trying to kill you!" It seemed to concern the game I was playing.

I did not see it on this occasion, from what I can remember, nor the games after it.

I remember when I saw this again when the original Xbox came out. My dad had bought it for me and hidden it in the closet in our living room.

Every night, I would open the closet and carefully take the Xbox out of the packaging to play a few games of FIFA.

Then, I would put it back neatly as I headed to bed.

The game I saw this on again was one I mentioned before: True Crime: Streets of L.A. In the game, you played a cop in the Los Angeles Police Department.

Along with the game, you collected good cop or bad cop points, depending on your actions during the game.

For example, shooting a hostage by accident would give you lousy cop points, as would arresting people on the street who weren't carrying contraband.

On the contrary, if you managed to stop someone on the street who did happen to have something on them, you would regain good cop points.

Too many lousy cop points, and you would be kicked off the force. As an inexperienced player of these third-person shooters, this happened to me pretty soon.

To get back on the police force, you had to regain enough good cop points until you were allowed to carry on with the game's missions and storyline.

This was difficult at first because once you were off the police force, the only way to regain good cop points was to search and arrest people on the sidewalk.

And because there seemed to be no way to tell if they were good or bad, you often got bad cop points even when the suspect looked like a drug dealer.

Although I soon found a method to always find a lousy suspect with contraband. I pointed my weapon at a passer-by, and if they put their hands in the air and stood still, I let them go. However, if they started running, I would chase after them and arrest them, always finding them guilty suspects.

I became good at the game after getting back on the police force. I ensured I didn't shoot any hostages by accident, which the bad guys often held at gunpoint.

After completing the game and beating the boss at the end, I decided to play the game on a harder difficulty.

I was playing it constantly, probably not sleeping at all.

After some determination and concentration, I completed the game again, but this time in hard mode.

Like many shooters, ending a game on hard mode unlocked an even more brutal version of the game, which you could play if you dared.

This one was called Insane.

It took me only a little while to complete the game again, on this new difficulty, I faced the alternative and more difficult showdown with the boss. Nonetheless, I was turning into a living vegetable.

I had lost weight since playing the game. There was little time for food because my eyes were glued to the screen. My thumbs and fingers were pressed against the Xbox controller constantly.

As I said previously, video gaming mush had begun etching its way across the black screen of the old cathode-ray tube television. The words were all too familiar to me:

The Kalvin Klein Conspiracy

I am trying to remember what happened afterwards, like if anything significant occurred. To clarify, on the first occasion with Grand Theft Auto, eventually, the screen blacked completely. At first, I suspected the parents in the kitchen could be to blame, so I investigated by knocking on the closed door and enquiring about it, but they had no idea.

With the Nokia phone, the mobile started working again shortly after that.

This was the next occurrence, in 2003, with a game my dad bought me called Lord of the Rings: Return of the King. The game came out in console formats, but my dad had bought it for my little grey computer.

The game was perfect, with interactive scenes from the actual movies, following the original film to its latest instalment in the trilogy.

The game worked because there was, besides the intense gameplay of orcs and tree beards, a separate screen of all the characters' faces in a nice-looking navigation screen. As you progressed through the game's missions, you unlocked more and more characters from the series, playing multiple different people from Tolkien's Middle Earth. There was no unlocking a secret difficulty mode with this. No, something different happened on this occasion.

I wanted to know how I did it or if other people experienced this with the game, but I found a way to unlock hidden characters further up the ladder after completing the general game. First, I unlocked the lesser-known hobbits Merry and Pippin and completed their challenges. Then came Boromir's brother, Faramir, unlocked, but the last character you unlocked was slightly ambiguous as to who it was. No doubt, it was Sean Bean, but the game said Boromir was Lord Sauron. It kind of made sense in that the fact that it didn't.

After not sleeping for so long as I constantly played this game and barely ate, without the nuisance of going to school, I was exhausted and even highly euphoric. After seeing Sean Bean, or Lord Sauron, the screen turned black pretty soon. Once more, I saw the following words, this time appearing on the old-fashioned chunky grey computer monitor:

The Kalvin Klein Conspiracy

The last time I saw these words was on an arcade Sniper game in Blackpool. When I was fourteen, I was on holiday with my dad. I was getting pretty good at the sniper game. It only took two attempts, which cost fifty pence each. Then I saw it again:

The Kalvin Klein Conspiracy

So what does all this mean? Had I hallucinated the words *The Kalvin Klein Conspiracy* appearing in the hacks of video, computer, and arcade games? Or was it some kind of easter egg that game developers put into the old games? Perhaps not.

Whatever the case, I stumbled across this term, *The Kalvin Klein Conspiracy*, through a hallucination of my own mind.

Still, I'm unsure whether I came up with the phrase before or after hallucinating these words in games. One thing is for sure, though, I had come up with strange stories, diagrams, and sketches before this, with characters like The Magician and Kalvin Klein entering the world I had created, a world I thought was real.

So pretty soon, these sketches and stories would return, and I would make a little comic book to bring to school, calling it *The Kalvin Klein Conspiracy*.

The story of the comic features the hallucination of the words *The Kalvin Klein Conspiracy* on the screens of the video games.

Ultimately, *The Kalvin Klein Conspiracy* sounds like something cool. It almost sounds like it is a real thing. In a way, it has become something. It is my childhood story which manifested back at itself, in a mentally ill-type way. It became the phrase I used to describe when a hallucination occurred. "Oh," I would say, "It's The Kalvin Klein Conspiracy at it again."

There will always be many Kalvin Kleins. It's a common name.

The story really had nothing to do with the fashion brand that shares the same name. Although clothing itself can represent a person's belief system. A person who wears all black all the time, perhaps with dark shades for sunglasses, is a person who feels out of place with the vast majority of the world. Such a person wears black to identify with an idea of non-conformity.

The idea was made apparent in the film *The Matrix*, where their free minds dress only in black when being jacked into the neural interactive simulation.

CHAPTER 4
HUNGER STRIKE

BEFORE I STARTED smoking cigarettes, I had a little fascination with fasting when I was younger.

I liked to secretly fast and drink only water. It wasn't about losing weight, although it was always a plus when I dropped a few pounds. It was never a good thing, though. I was just little, and I didn't understand.

I remember this one occasion where I fasted for about a month, just before my thirteenth birthday.

My dad was out doing something on my birthday, and I was at home, in the bathroom, filling up a two-litre bottle of water.

I gulped down all of the water without taking a break. After not eating for so long, it gave me a great rush to drink cold water like this. Every day I would come home to my dad's dinner, throwing the food away. It was a bit ungrateful, but he never suspected as much.

I didn't know I was suffering from a mental health condition. I didn't have an eating disorder.

A mental health professional said many people have experienced some form of an eating disorder in some phase of their life.

I drank so much water and felt like my belly had expanded from the sheer amount. I stood on the old weighing scales in the bathroom, hallucinating something strange. I looked at the number on the scale, and it had gone entirely to the right as if I was a morbidly obese person.

These were old scales my dad had from a long time ago, and the amount they go up is very high. I could not have possibly weighed so much just from drinking a lot of water.

That made no sense. Besides, I was only thirteen and had just gone without eating. If anything, I should be weighing less and less, not this hallucinatory amount.

The water was too much, though, the sickness came, and I began vomiting water into the toilet. The water didn't stop coming out of me until I was completely emptied and left with a severe migraine.

I retreated to bed and tried to subdue the pain in my head, which was excruciating and seemed to stretch to every inch of my body. When my dad came home, I came downstairs and stood before him. I understand that human memory is constructive and false because what I remember couldn't have possibly happened. I remember some transformation took place. I shrank to the size of a five-year-old. It happened in a split second, but this recollection is a symptom of a mental disorder.

Whilst unwell, I believed it for a long time, and many things like this. Now I'm well. I can see how the human memory is unreliable, especially in an instance such as this when I have been suffering from early psychosis.

As we get to this part of the memory, the whole thing becomes unreliable, but in this memoir, I shall tell you what I used to believe about what happened. It was my birthday, and a classmate from school came around to visit me. I lost control of my arm and punched him in the cheek.

He went home, and I'm sorry, but this probably didn't happen anyway. I have a false memory of losing conscious control of my arm, and I have this memory of someone else being in control of the movement of my limbs.

It has been a strange life to live and believe in these memories of the past. There is some truth to it: I probably did have a slight problem with eating during some short periods.

However, the way I remember everything is not reliable at all. I write this merely to demonstrate insight into my mental health.

I once posted a stupid idea about The Matrix and The Truman Show on Facebook. I was so upset with myself that the feeling of shame was almost too much.

I often get that feeling with social media, but it's usually during an unwell phase.

So, in a hallucination while watching The Truman Show, I thought I saw the screen split to the image of Brad Pitt on the screen.

I didn't see this hallucination for that long, to be quite fair.

There are two things I heard the hallucination of Brad Pitt's voice say, though.

These are the words I heard him say:

Better pick up that shovel.

My dad probably still remembers why I was standing outside the Co Op that day with a shovel, but I just decided to get some Lucozade when I got there.

The other thing the hallucination of Brad Pitt that came through on audio after the short split of the screen was this:

What does curb can man drink?

It appeared convincing, and people didn't understand how real it came across.

Now I want to tell you about the time my father and I saw a guy who looked just like Brad Pitt. A lot of what the psychiatrists call hallucination appears on the television or computer, but there are many aspects I remember which just happened in the realm of real life.

The strange thing about this, although perhaps not the events of the second time, but my father, the sane man, remembers seeing this guy too. If it wasn't Brad Pitt, then it must have been some kind of clone, because it really was the spitting image of him. Yet this is a story which led up to this too, and here I tell it to you.

When I was a kid, there were periods when I used to starve myself, almost half to death sometimes.

It's something I can't do anymore. Especially on medications like antipsychotics, like a nurse said to me once in the hospital, "You are going to feel the sedation a lot more."

Sometimes I found when I didn't eat for a long time, I wouldn't sleep either.

Sometimes I would see the most extraordinary situations. Sometimes actors and movies would come alive on the screen, seemingly as if they were in the same room as me, like it had all become live, hyperreal, and uncanny. I've seen aspects of this nature on medication, after I've left the hospital, even in the hospital, just not to the nature and degree of the crazy days of my adolescence. Even music artists come into this sphere of paranoid schizophrenia. None of it makes much sense, but it feels so real when you see or hear stuff like this, and it makes you want to see it all again. It makes you want to "gain access" to it, but you know it's unlikely you will ever be able to show the world about this very world you have seen. You won't be able to prove it. Essentially, you admit defeat and say, "This is my schizophrenia. This is what it is like for me," and it's not a negative experience. It's all been enlightening when you see it emerge on the computer or television.

I don't actually have an eating disorder. I said before, I remember them diagnosing me with paranoid schizophrenia in my early youth, and at the same time, I remember the same doctor diagnosing me with EDNOS. That means eating disorder not otherwise specified, and it usually is a combination of anorexia, bulimia, and binge-eating disorder. But that doesn't matter because it's not in the current spectrum of my notes, and like every other aspect which you may call a delusion, I ascribe it to a part of The Kalvin Klein Conspiracy.

A healthcare assistant called Jerry, in the local adult ward called Applewood in my hometown, tells me that most people experience some kind of eating disorder at some point in their lives. In the beginning, I was just starving myself out of stubbornness and a desire to be really thin, but later I found myself doing this as an active measure to search out elements of the Conspiracy. I know we haven't yet discussed much of the material I have actually seen emerging, but really, it can be anything. Most of the time, it seems to be a deleted scene, but even if you were to look in the extras on any product, you would still never find what you had seen.

At our primary school, the teachers give us little red-coloured New Testaments with gold lining on the side of the pages, so when you close it, the side of it looks golden. Our headteacher told us all to read it, but I only read about as far as when Jesus is fasting in the desert and is tempted by the devil. It must have had some kind of effect on me because when I tried to starve myself, I was always going for the golden number of forty days and forty nights. When you get punched in the face at school on a four-week empty stomach, then you find out you can't really take that punch. Most people fasting don't expect to get hit, but when you do after such a long period of starvation, for some reason, the punch just hurts a lot more than usual.

It was my thirteenth birthday, and I had gone a long time without eating. How long exactly, I can't be sure. I used to drink a lot of water when I went through these starvation periods. Water tasted great when you didn't eat for a long time. That's when I began drinking more and more water. It was pretty disgusting, but I kept on getting a two-litre empty bottle and filling it up with tap water. Then I guzzled it down as fast as I could, without a break.

I seemed to get some kind of rush out of this and kept on doing it repeatedly until I was so full, my belly had completely expanded from the dangerous amount of water I had consumed. I was full and tight.

As I stood on the scales, something strange happened. The little ticker on the measurement of the scales just went to the full mark. On the bottom of the scales, it read *Property of MOD*, so my dad must have gotten them when he was in the army. This was impossible. You know how much these old industrial scales go up to? There was no way I could have drunk so much water that I now weighed that much. Yet, that is what I saw that day. Perhaps I was vividly hallucinating in the bathroom. You may say it was from the starvation or the mental illness itself, but to me, this is just what I remember clearly, and to me, the reality we live in is just a description. Sometimes it's hard to write a story or a memoir with unbelievable elements coming to light all the time, but I endeavour to explain all this in terms of the mental health condition. My life is hard because I question how I can go on with my day-to-day life when I've seen all this abstract material and situations come to life.

I began throwing up the water involuntarily into the toilet. I may as well have been projectile vomiting because that was how much was coming out of me. As I kept on trying to repeatedly flush the toilet, it kept on filling up really fast because so much water was departing from me now. A lot of water and acidity came out of me, but then as you tried to drink some more, to try and replace some lost fluid and help restore the electrolyte balance, this just made me throw up even more. It was a vicious cycle I had brought upon myself. My head was hurting badly now, so I retreated to the bedroom and hid underneath the covers.

These headaches were bad. They were worse than migraines. It felt like an eagle had its claw inside my brain and was digging it out of my ear. I began to scream sometimes because it hurt so much. I was thirteen years old, and I was scared. I hadn't eaten in a very long time, and now I had done something stupid with the water. I don't know what possessed me to do it, but at first, the influx of water felt great after being empty for so long.

As I lay there in pain, I thought to myself no one would ever believe how much this hurt. I thought I was going to die. I thought my head was going to explode. Every time I focused on my breathing and thought I had the pain in my head under control, it would come back with vengeance.

The only thing comparable to this pain I felt that day was when my best friend at primary school convinced me to use my broken arm in a cast as a blunt object to hit him over the head with. That wasn't very clever, and man, did it hurt a great deal. I tried to explain to the teacher that I had broken my arm again, but she just kept on saying she already knew my arm was in a cast. I ended up screaming like a little girl until the headmaster came and made me explain exactly why I was in so much pain, then she took me to A&E to get re-casted and some pain relief.

I remember being thirteen and lying in my bed with the excruciating pain in my head, and lying numb for a few moments as the pain eased, although it would be back, I could think to myself, "I'm still here. I'm still Kalvin Klein," I think just before I thought this is when I first changed in size. This is perhaps another element of the memoir you would ascribe to delusional thinking, as it now becomes apparent.

I remember it happening on several different occasions during the crazy periods of my adolescence. I even remember it happening with a friend of mine from school. Back then, I always called it metamorphosis in my line of thinking because I didn't know what else to call it. It's just a matter of shrinking, or in some cases, the opposite of shrinking, turning from a young boy into the state of a fully-grown man. I remember situations and events like this happening so vividly in my memory, somewhere deep inside me, I know I will never go back on my own mind and think to myself that none of this is real. On one hand, we understand it in terms of the mental health condition. From your point of view, you may see that sometimes people with such a condition simply believe things that clearly aren't true, but on the other hand, it's just quite plain and simple to me, very real.

Back then, my dad had the habit of yelling my name when coming home through the back door of the house. I came down immediately and stood in front of him in the narrow kitchen. I was fairly short as a thirteen-year-old kid, but when the so-called metamorphosis happens, it just happens, very quickly and like an electric bolt through your whole body. Now I was standing in front of him about the height of when I was five.

I know if I asked my father, he wouldn't remember this. Despite that, I still remember this, and I remember my dad looking at me from across the hallway and saying to me, "How are you doing this?"

The pain in the head was still coming and going. I'm not exaggerating at all, this was unbearable pain. I kept screaming in bed, so eventually, my dad took me to Marlborough House. This is where I was when I was about thirteen. Like the instance in Beechleydene with the allergic reaction to peanut butter, this wasn't recorded by the mental health service. They gave me a shot of morphine in the clinic room.

They put me on the electronic scales. It said I weighed *zero*. Then, in front of the staff, I levitated, just slightly above the scales, in the air for a moment. I know you don't believe people can levitate or fly, but this is just simply what I distinctly remember in terms of the condition I'm experiencing. I remember other times in my natural memory of levitation off the ground as well. Last year, I was in an argument with my father at his house. Where he sits, there is a computer against the door with a British flag draped over it so he can't see me on the other side. But as I get angry, I also realize I'm walking on thin air, and all I can think to myself is, "Typical, my dad can't see because he is behind a door with a thick flag over it."

What happened that day felt real to me, like the stress of the moment had caused me to fly slightly off the ground. On one hand, we look at this in terms of someone suffering a mental health condition because no one believes anyone can fly, but on the other hand, if somehow I wake up from the madness of reality one day and all these elements of the *Conspiracy* come true, then I would be able to learn to fly, although most of the time I conclude that this is just a harsh and terrible world we live in, and the chances of any of this coming true would make me the luckiest man alive.

The day I received a shot of morphine at Marlborough House, there was no assessment or doctors, that was simply it, and then my father took me home. It was still my birthday, so my dad suggested he call a friend to come around. The boy I know from school is standing there at the end of the kitchen, and he looks weary at the sight of me as I stand at the other end of the kitchen. He's probably surprised at how much weight I've lost. Neither of us spoke to each other that day. Sometimes when I don't sleep for more than five days, I feel like someone else is taking over my body.

It was like Kalvin Klein had taken over that part of my arm that day and just decided to hit that kid from school. Although with Kalvin, there is no story of the mental health experience for me, at the same time, the way I remember Kalvin, as a different part of my personality, well, he wasn't a very nice person.

My father decides to take us for a trip to Bath.

Before we left Swindon, we stopped at a little convenience shop, and I go inside to buy one of those cheap 20p drinks with a straw in it, the type you can't really get anymore. When I bought my drink, I asked the shop clerk how old he thought I was, and he replied hopefully, "Five?" in question.

"I'm thirteen years old, I'll have you know," I yelled at him.

We stopped at a Motorway Station to get a pound-saver hamburger at McDonald's.

It had gone past the idea of starving myself now. I was willing to eat something because I didn't want the pain in my head to return, which since the shot of morphine, seemed to only come in slight twinges.

This is the part my father remembers too.

We are standing there in an empty McDonald's. Usually, such a place wouldn't be empty, but maybe this was because it was the side of the motorway.

The strangest thing was that he seemed to be working there. He was wearing the full uniform, even the hats they used to wear back then. At the time, their uniforms were green a lot in colour. This didn't just look similar to Brad Pitt. This guy was his spitting image. The tan, the face, the dimples, and the all-American grin wiped across his face, like he was expecting us. My dad couldn't believe it and turns to me, saying, "Isn't that... but... how?" He was perplexed. I just smiled, like I knew what was going on.

At that age, I wasn't much of a Brad Pitt fan. I've seen more of his films as an adult.

Back then, the only film I had seen of his was Legends of the Fall because this was quite a common family film at the time, and my dad even covered my eyes during the love scenes. I was aware of the name though; it was floated here and there about, in the name of Shania Twain's song, on an episode of Mary-Kate and Ashley, or whoever your sister fancied at that time. I recognized him immediately though in the McDonald's restaurant.

Somewhere in my schizophrenic mind, I had got the film Legends of the Fall and Secret Garden mixed up. These are the type of family films you watch on your VHS player when you are a kid, along with A Little Princess and Chitty Chitty Bang-Bang. I thought the character called Tristan comes back at the end of Secret Garden and says to his son, "Of course, I'm real," then like in Legends of the Fall, he directs all the wild horses to come back onto the ranch in a massive wave, except he is directing them to come back onto the grounds near the mansion where Secret Garden is set. The truth is I don't know about this, but with other aspects, sometimes a distinct change in a scene of a film, or sometimes an entire film which simply doesn't exist or appear to, comes to light, and it feels not only as real as watching other normal stuff, it feels more real than real, like something has come alive on screen. It becomes hyperreal.

I've seen a small movie listed on the Internet Movie Database described as *Man Who Finds a Brad Pitt Cloning Centre*. I can't remember the name of the film though, and typing it into the search engine *Brad Pitt cloning centre film* only brings up some weird results.

My father and I sat down and ate our hamburgers, even though if you really think about it, we should have gone and approached this guy who looked just like Brad Pitt. It happened in such a strange fashion though, that we just thought to sit down for a moment and perhaps see him later.

Music was playing in the background of the restaurant. It was the song by James Blunt called *Beautiful*. It's a nice song, but at the time, it was really doing my head in. It was bringing back the twinge of unbearable pain inside my head, so I yelled out an expletive that rhymed with Blunt's last name. At this point, the manager of the restaurant came out, a skinny guy with rectangular glasses dressed in black trousers and a white shirt.

This is when we realized Brad Pitt was no longer to be seen serving behind the counter. The manager asked if I could not use such language because sometimes there might be kids there. My dad didn't want me to say anything about the actor we had just come across under these unusual circumstances, so as not to sound crazy. I don't know what my dad thought at the time, but it's interesting to see how he still remembers this part of the story even to this day. He rationalizes it though and says the guy was just a lookalike. Even if that is true, I can't stress how much this guy looked exactly like the actor. If you have seen the images of such lookalikes on the internet, then you know they don't exactly look like replicas of the actor, but this guy did.

My father remembers the B&B we stayed at, but he doesn't remember seeing a so-called lookalike there again. Nonetheless, this is how I remember it.

At the small hotel, not far from the cathedral, the manager is always standing at the front desk in his suit, and my father is in our room. I ventured out into the hallway to feast my eyes upon something. Now I can see Brad Pitt standing there in normal clothing, with a visible Hollywood haircut, and he seems to be talking with the manager of the B&B, but he hasn't noticed me yet.

Standing there in the hallway, it felt like I was really in the presence of a huge actor, and I didn't want to waste my opportunity like I had done at McDonald's. It didn't matter in my mind what the hell Brad Pitt was doing at a shoddy B&B in the middle of Bath because I could see him with my eyes. I yelled it in a stringy American accent that you sometimes hear a little kid annoyingly put on, "Kalvin Klein!" and whoever this guy was seemed aghast at this.

He starts yelling at the B&B manager, "How did he know that? How the fuck did he know that?"

If they were lookalikes, what are the chances of running into two of them in such odd places on the same day, in quick succession? I wasn't hallucinating Brad Pitt like out of a scene from a movie either. My father had seen him at the restaurant and here at the B&B. The way I remember, he was talking to the hotel manager. I thought it had something to do with the starvation and the water. I always liked to think it was the real Brad Pitt, but perhaps towards the end of this story, it seems more likely to have been a lookalike, no matter how much he looked just like him.

Later on, as the day turns into the night slowly, this Brad Pitt guy is sitting outside in the back garden of the hotel with the defunct pool, with a woman who kind of looks like Angelina Jolie. I remember thinking that she was way too short to be the real Angelina, but it's not as though I know how tall that person is. And she was white as snow in her complexion. Her eyes were huge, like she was an alien. I don't know if they were dating at the time, but it was around 2005. She says to me, "We'll adopt you."

I told her I already had a family. That night, the Brad Pitt guy didn't open his mouth to talk once. I had heard him in the corridor, but after this, he seemed to be annoyed at my presence. He just sat there, with eyes staring into the horizon, like it was a scene out of a movie. The Angelina girl spoke sometimes, and I kept on speaking to them at great lengths, but there is no way in my mind I can recollect what I said that night. In a way, you remember everything, but such a phrase is just an expression. You don't remember what you had for breakfast two years ago on this exact day.

This might sound weird, but I remember this Brad Pitt beating the hell out of me, except it didn't hurt at all. Just like the aspect of the metamorphosis, it happened fast, too fast to be real, like a lightning bolt. Before I went to bed, this Angelina Jolie woman gives me a big smackeroo on the side of my cheek, leaving the wet, red imprint of a kiss mark. When I return to our room, my father sees that I have been beat up and goes outside to confront whoever he may find, but soon he just returns moments later, with a kiss mark on his cheek too.

In the morning, I don't see them, but I know they are eating breakfast in a separate room from us. I was crying. Even though I was thirteen, I looked a lot younger that day. I was crying because I thought it was the real Brad Pitt and that he wouldn't speak to me or give me his autograph. I was crying because of all that starvation. Before the morning was out, though, whoever this guy was did give me some kind of autograph.

This is what makes me think it must have been some kind of remarkable lookalike that just happened to look identical to the real star. You could make a lot of money looking that similar to these kinds of actors, but you'd think it would be on the internet more. I remember our family thought we met George Clooney on holiday in Spain once. That guy looked exactly like George Clooney, although as he explained, he just made a living off looking identical to George Clooney, or so he told us.

I remember my thoughts in Spain when I met him. I told myself it was the real George Clooney, and this was just his cover story.

On the napkin, this guy had just written "BRAD PITT" just like that, in capital letters, with a marker pen. Obviously, this wasn't a real autograph.

If it was the real actor, then he would have given a real autograph. You could argue that it would have been too hard to write that on a napkin with a marker pen, but it seemed like a poor excuse to not go and find a pen and a piece of paper. Even though it wasn't the real actor, it was still remarkable what happened. Looking at these guys we saw that day, you would think if they weren't the real actor, then they looked so much like him that they must have been clones. Even if my dad didn't remember the events that happened at the B&B, he still remembers the strange circumstances we saw this guy at McDonald's. If there was a guy who looked like this working at McDonald's, everyone would know about it. He looked identical to the real guy. It would be in the news, people would take photographs, but despite all this, my dad still, at least, admits he remembers this part of my story, of this strange mental health experience of mine. Most of it was sleep deprivation that manifested because of my mental health condition, schizoaffective disorder.

The burger was in my belly, and the pangs in my head were still there. The hunger strike was all over.

But don't take my word for it. Drink coffee and stay awake night after night. I don't advocate cigarettes, despite chain-smoking while I wrote this, but you could have a vape. Then, after you build up some sleep deprivation, put on your favourite movie and watch as you get sucked into a Warner Bros honey hive logo of Looney Tunes.

End up in some annoying real live version of a film scenario of a story like The Haunting until you find a way to make it the land of The Walking Dead.

Obviously, that isn't possible or recommended.

Don't wholly knock what I'm saying before you have experienced it yourself.

I don't actually recommend anyone experience what I have experienced through sleep deprivation and the resulting hallucinations.

You don't have to take my word for it, but just consider what I tell you.

Sometimes, mental health professionals have a good understanding of this.

Some of my family significantly understand how I saw all this, even though it would not be possible to be seen by others.

Once again, it may not have been real, but to my mind, it has always appeared real.

Appearing just as real as anything else, like the cup of coffee you can hold in the morning or the school you used to go to as a kid. Seemingly as real as death and taxes, that's for sure.

I hate to say it, but it is like what Morpheus says in The Matrix:

"Unfortunately, no one can be told what The Matrix is. They have to see it for themselves."

The only difference is I'm talking about hallucinations. Most people don't know what it is like to see hallucinations like this.

You would have to see it for yourself. I'm not saying there can't be empathy or sympathy, far from it, but I don't require that at all, nor would I want that.

What would you do?

I didn't do research into actual studies of hallucinations or mental health. I didn't want this to be boring. I'm not speaking about mental health on those terms because I'm not giving advice.

My effort has been to give the mental health narrative from the perspective of the person going through the hard times.

Some people might need to learn what I mean when I say mind. Other people may disagree with my definition of mind, which is simply a philosophical mind that science doesn't have a way of conceiving in its existence. It has been good to have my dad by my side. He is someone of sound mind and has a lot of experience in different lines of life, so when confronted by the psychiatric services, it gives me some breathing room to have someone stick up for me a bit. No one is perfect, but my dad is a pretty cool guy. I think with this occurrence of a Brad Pitt type character, my mind was thinking it was like a futuristic android or cyborg, which had somehow been sent back to that exact time, as he masqueraded as a McDonald's clerk. Well, my imagination was running away with me again. It makes for an interesting plot in a story but in the real world, it was probably just Brad Pitt's evil twin brother.

CHAPTER 5
HELL ON EARTH

THE HALLUCINATIONS HAVE been a mixture of sweetness and torture. I remember growing up thinking this occurred on television, but I have seen the show correctly, and what I saw never happened. It was a TV show called Smallville with Tom Welling. Lana and Clark were at the football game, and Lana said, "Clark, you are not allowed to use your powers in the football match." Some football players were seriously injured. Clark said, "I didn't."

With the music of the show Smallville, I had always thought Kelly Osbourne sang that song because that is precisely what I used to listen to on YouTube, but now it is all gone and was just hallucinations. The song was called *Save Me*, and it was actually by Remy Zero. I have been tortured by these hallucinations, but at the same time, I still miss them, but I realize I can never go that far back in my wellness. I'm doing quite well.

I saw a hallucination on television with Adam Sandler on a bus in modest clothing. He was wearing a green parka and a pair of blue jeans. The song was playing, *What if God was one of us? On a bus like one of us. Trying to make his way home.* I thought the trailer was a joke. The song that I heard in the hallucination was by Joan Osborne. I don't think everyone will understand this memoir because some people think I'm making these hallucinations up for a laugh. It wasn't an advertisement at all, but I guess, being a kid back then, I just thought it was. It took me all my life to recognize these as hallucinations. As a kid, I stared at these hallucinations and tried not to talk about them. I was worried that people would find out what I could see. This is not that strange at all. Although people's experiences may be vastly different, mental health problems happen like this every single day. It's more common than some people want to make out. This memoir is about the conversation in mental health, bringing it to the foreground and saying to everyone, here it is. If mental health is to be talked about, then I'm being honest about it.

Then again, the hallucination never said it was anything to do with the film Little Nicky. My mind just always made that connection. Movies used to affect me because of my mental health condition. All I can offer is my ability to be honest here. All I can do regarding these hallucinations is concentrate on not seeing them anymore. I have to get on with things.

I was watching the original Superman film. I saw Superman, dressed in his costume, hanging around in an alleyway and smoking a cigarette. This doesn't happen in the movie. A character in the film was playing the reporter role with an old-fashioned camera. When Superman smoked the cigarette, it made his eyes glow red. He became angry at the reporter for taking snaps at him, so he destroyed his camera, pushing the guy to the floor. I don't think the human mind is supposed to experience hallucinations. When I was a kid, I didn't like comic books. Then I saw hallucinations, unknowingly they were hallucinations. I became interested in comic books. It's like I have been cursed with the pictorial form, originating from caveman days. I picture cavemen writing numbers on walls, giving lessons to me. I look at myself, and I can't believe I started smoking as a teenager.

All I want in this life is to give it all up. The tobacco, the caffeine, and even watching television. I want it all to go in the end, so I can focus on my mind and mental health. If psychiatry doesn't recognize the mind being authentic in my philosophical sense, then that is a simple agree-to-disagree notion.

I will always talk to psychiatry on a rational basis. That's what civilized society is all about—people sit down and talk to each other. Sometimes it can be avoided to exhaustion, but I don't blame anyone for avoiding it.

The Departed film is mentioned in this memoir. It is unfortunate because it is such a good film. A guy on YouTube called Michael Franzese talks about the nature of the film. To some, there is no difference between cops and criminals. I see the point clearly; cops and criminals aren't always best friends, but they are sometimes part of the same life. In some instances, police work with criminals. Even occasionally, a criminal goes to work for an agency like the FBI. It just comes down to everyone being a human being.

I was around 14 years old when I experienced this full-blown hallucination.

It involved a film called Hell on Earth: 666, which starred Eric Balfour. It didn't really star Eric Balfour because it was a hallucination. Unlike the previous hallucinations, this specific film didn't even exist.

I first saw this on the television in my dad's living room. Dad was out somewhere.

We had Freeview back in those days, and when I pressed the button on the remote, the menu would come up on the screen, showing the show's name.

The show's name appeared as Hell on Earth, but to either the left or right-hand side, the 6s seemed to go on forever. This is what it looked like:

6666666 Hell on Earth 6666666

The numbers continued right to the edge of where the television screen ended. Imagine what my mind must have thought.

I didn't know what to think. I thought that because it was seemingly playing on every channel on Freeview, it might have been a broadcast that was going out. I wondered if other people in other houses were viewing the same thing. At the same time, I knew I couldn't mention this to anyone because I was keen enough to realize that, in all probability, no one else was seeing this.

Mentioning it to anyone would just make me out to be crazy by society's standards. That was definitely the gist of how I thought about the hallucinations when I was younger.

I wanted to know where the television show was being broadcast and how. Most of the time as a kid, I never considered them hallucinations. That was like a phoney idea to my young mind. The way I saw the hallucinations in my youth was that they were a fantastic phenomenon that ended up in my field of vision.

I grew up, and as I experienced problems in my mental health, I began to recognize the hallucinations for what they were.

At the time, I still wondered why and how it appeared to be playing on every Freeview channel, no matter how many times I switched.

There wasn't much to the first time I saw Hell on Earth: 666.

Eric Balfour and his blond-haired best friend were standing on a city sidewalk, staring right back at the camera.

As I watched this hallucination on the television, I noticed Eric Balfour's character was wearing a red leather jacket, just like Brad Pitt's character wears in Fight Club.

The place they were in, with lit-up stores at night, was similar to the imaginary Portland area in which the film Fight Club is set.

I remember from this first hallucination that Eric Balfour's character and his friend were talking but looking directly at the screen. Nothing was said, but watching hallucinations like this can be fascinating. They can also drive people, such as myself, mad at the same time.

Sometimes, I quickly forget what I have just dreamt when I wake up from a dream. The hallucinations were like dreams in my waking life.

I had stayed awake for five days on this occasion.

As a kid, I called this *The Bargain of Five Days*. My unwell idea was that if I stayed awake for five days, I would surely get what I was looking for in terms of the hallucinations. In my unwellness, I thought I could capture and show what was happening to the world.

Social media interested me because I thought I would post it there.

As a kid, I never had a camera phone; as an adult, it made no difference anyway.

I was crazy in my youth and even in adulthood when I considered what I saw as anything other than pure hallucination.

Another time I experienced this Hell on Earth: 666 hallucination was when I was 15 years old. I feel so bad for myself, just being such a gullible kid, even in terms of my fragile mind. I believe in myself, though, and believe my mind is stronger because of it now. I don't think the mind is an illusion, but there is an illusion of the mind's power sometimes.

The hallucination came back as a whole film I watched on my laptop.

I knew it was the same Hell on Earth: 666 hallucination because it starred Eric Balfour again with his blond-haired best friend.

I had purposely deprived myself of sleep to see the world of hallucinations. I admit this was foolish, and as I live my days, rest is the most crucial thing in my life. Without it, a guy like me couldn't tie his own shoelaces properly or attempt to write a bare-bones memoir like this.

The film also starred Eric Balfour's character's blond-haired girlfriend and her brunette-haired best friend.

The hair colours were all I had to go by because I didn't recognize these actors. I watched these hallucinations but failed to pick up on any of the characters' names.

All four of these characters were traveling to a party at a warehouse. It was like some urban rave.

On the way back, they all started to argue and then, as they did, they crashed into another car and spun off the side of the road. It's bad enough to see such things in movies. For some, imagine what it is like to see it in a hallucination when I didn't know what was going on.

The accident killed the blond-haired characters and left Eric and the mean girl alive.

So Eric Balfour's character had lost his girlfriend and best friend, all in one car crash.

Eric and the brunette girl became the film's subject matter as Eric Balfour's character's life slowly became a living hell.

The brunette girl manipulated him and said mean, terrible things to him.

The main character, played by the hallucinatory Eric Balfour, kept seeing his dead girlfriend and friend calling out to him.

He thought it was them calling out to him from the after all.

Towards the film's end, he wakes up in a hospital after being in a coma.

His blond-haired amigos are actually by the side of his hospital bed and had been calling out to him.

I always thought it was not the best ending to the film, despite it being an unreal hallucination. Like my headteacher said at Gilbert's Hill, don't end the story with the phrase, "It was just a dream." I don't think my hallucination was that creative on this occasion. I just write about the hallucinations in this memoir. I don't actually choose what I see.

I think the name of the hallucinatory film was about the main character's life, as it had become a living hell until he woke up from that nightmare.

Someone with a mental health problem often has so much potential, and it seems unfair that sometimes that potential is wasted when it could be expressed just like this in a book or through another medium.

In my youth, I had a bad attitude regarding watching hallucinations. I said to myself, "Well, I know other people can't see this. So maybe I will sit here and watch as much as possible."

I still find the nature of hallucinations complicated to understand. After all, what is real?

According to Morpheus in The Matrix, what is real is just electrical signals interpreted by the brain. I have always found that phrase to be the most enlightening philosophy.

I think a major point in the simulation hypothesis would be that the brain would not be in a vat but would be part of the simulation. I think it's intriguing, but I genuinely hold true to a more mathematical interpretation of life.

I think The Matrix has lots of metaphors, but the assertion about electrical signals in the brain rings most true.

Something I've always believed in is perspective.

Your mind makes it real. If you really believe something, then it can affect you, for good or for bad.

CHAPTER 6
USUAL HALLUCINATIONS

ONE TIME, I was watching Road Trip, and I hallucinated an alien humanoid person. She was female, and she had an enormous forehead. I felt so attracted to this hallucinatory alien.

She looked just like a beautiful woman with an overtly prominent forehead. I saw it as a youngster that aliens have big foreheads, making them more attractive, with bigger brains, and therefore must be much better in bed than humans. It definitely wasn't in the usual course of the film.

During this time, I also saw a young angel appear from Return to Oz on YouTube, the one with blond hair, but I found this hallucination annoying, and I couldn't remember a word that the hallucination angel said. It was a long time ago.

I didn't like this hallucination at all. I don't think people understand how addictive hallucinating like this can be.

The thing about the alien hallucination was that you would have to see it to know what I was talking about. If other people saw it, they would have come to the same conclusion before chucking it off as yet another crazed hallucination.

The next hallucination was to do with The Usual Suspects.

These are the hallucinations of my youth. A lot of the hallucinations occurred during most of my teenage years between fifteen and sixteen. In the film, I saw Michael Penn as the investigating policeman.

While questioning Kevin Spacey's character, Verbal Kint, he even said in my hallucination, "Something is rotten in Denmark."

It was strange because I had never seen this film before at first.

I didn't know Michael Penn wasn't in the movie.

The investigating detective is played by an actor called Chazz Palminteri, which I found out later.

I can't remember Michael Penn's version of the detective's in-depth conversations with Kevin Spacey, but I'm sure it differed significantly from the film's discussions.

I remember they kept on taking sips of black coffee.

Immediately, I went and grabbed myself a cup of coffee.

I rewound the movie for a few minutes to replay what they were saying.

It was weird. They were saying different things. I didn't say I have an exact photographic memory for every little thing, and given that I was going without sleep during the hallucinations, it's cool that I have bothered to remember any of this.

I remember my thoughts as a young man just clearly. I was sitting there thinking I had seen an alternative movie version. I found this so easy to believe because the hallucinatory version with Michael Penn just seemed to be a much more remarkable film to my mentally unwell mind.

When I was a kid, I watched those hallucinations and said, "Haha, no one else can see this but me." Even as a kid, though, most of the time, I didn't want to hallucinate. It just kept on happening.

As a young man, I still thought that when I saw these hallucinations, they were Titan AI Machines trying to tempt me in some form. I knew they weren't real. This is why I have written this memoir. It's my fault I hallucinated, which comes down to unhealthy thought patterns and staying up too late.

Titan AI Machines were sneaking into reality by showing themselves openly to me in movies?

It's not good to hallucinate. It makes a person believe strange things.

I thought I was being tempted. I'm just not sure what for. Perhaps I wasn't, but the hallucinations always suggested wild thought patterns. My brain didn't fully understand.

There was bitterness when I wrote about this, but I have watered it down somewhat. A purpose of the memoir is to display a side of mental health problems that don't necessarily go away for everyone.

I don't wish this on anyone. It scares me.

I just want to watch a horror movie and be normal for once.

I'm aware of my mental health problem and just want to take it easy.

When I was younger, I read about a mock religion in America called The Church of the SubGenius. They had some strange things to say, and I was drawn to their outrageous claims.

I managed to get my hands on a barrage DVD from the internet. I had no money as a teenager, so I asked my dad to buy this cool DVD because it might have a bonus on it.

I had seen the footage before on the web, but I wanted to know if it had any additional features on the DVD.

It was like a mental health worker once told me, "You shall go to the ball."

The speaker on the television in the film They Live is also in this SubGenius movie.

He narrates, and then you see him towards the film's end.

As I watched, this speaker first said under no circumstances should I turn the DVD over and watch the other side, even if anyone, including him, later in the DVD, states that I should. As the DVD went on, the speaker changed his mind and said I should turn over the DVD and watch it.

Despite what he warned about, I decided to see what lay on the other side of this double-sided DVD.

What I saw was a hallucination. I saw my dad and me on the video, who, at the time, I lived with.

We were like ourselves, but both were in top physical condition, and we were rogue cops. We looked cool, but it wasn't my dad or me.

The SubGenius DVD has a load of crazy footage and a speaker in the film warning viewers not to turn over the DVD.

However, whatever was meant to be on the other side of the manufactured double-sided DVD was not meant to be a hallucination of my dad and me.

Once again, my dad appeared in my hallucinations. I have an understanding parent. Otherwise, this would all be slightly more difficult to write about.

If you are reading this and have experienced similar or some form of hallucinations like these, I encourage you to share your story with the world. I do understand, though. People have a choice about anything they do in this life.

People shy away from talking about these aspects of mental health. It shouldn't be this way.

It is good to be open-minded, and we should feel free to express ourselves, even if it is an expression of a previously unwell state of mind.

It wasn't all negative. Sleep deprivation is no spring chicken, but I saw another world that may not exist.

The old SubGenius books always had humorous things to read about.

There was a suggestion in their main book that a person could see a parallel universe on television. That's the stupidest idea ever when taken too seriously.

With the way technology advances, it is possible that in the future, hallucinations may be detectable by AI. This is highly interesting, and artificial intelligence is doing wonders in the world now. Even more so in the future, AI will reduce the world's suffering.

Halloween was always a time to hallucinate. My dad was in this hallucination again. He was in some horror movie on the Freeview channels. I just remember seeing my dad on the television, walking about hastily at night, near these extensive gardens and hedgerows, and he was holding an axe in his hands. Sometimes my recollection of the hallucination is rather vague. Other times, it is more detailed due to certain factors. Those factors are merely down to memory and how the hallucination impacted me. In a way, calling all of it The Kalvin Klein Conspiracy helped me remember what was going on. I didn't fully know I was hallucinating due to the mental illness. However, I did know it was important to be observant of what I saw.

I had quite a few hallucinations of Star Wars during my teenage years. The first instance was when I was watching a Lord of the Rings movie during an episode of extreme sleep deprivation.

One of those rare moments during the hallucinations was when I sat there and thought, "Obviously, I'm hallucinating."

I don't want to come to terms with it too much anymore. I laugh at it all.

At that time, I still believed what I saw looked cool.

That's the real danger of the hallucinations, thinking they look so cool.

I just wanted more and more of the hallucinations.

Then there was The Two Towers film in the Lord of the Rings trilogy, and the Imperial March from Star Wars played as Darth Vader marched about in the distance of the footage I was seeing Darth Vader, leading an army of orcs towards some grand entrance on the horizon.

I wondered what Darth Vader was doing in the Lord of the Rings movie. My hallucination had got the wrong evil ruler this time. In Lord of the Rings, it is supposed to be Sauron, not Vader.

Another time during these teenage years, I watched the Phantom of the Menace. I saw the original Obi-Wan Kenobi, played by Alec Guinness from A New Hope, appear in this modern film.

At the film's beginning, he comments on the young Anakin Skywalker. He said, "The Force is strong with this one."

It was undoubtedly strange but fantastic to see this hallucination, especially as it was the original Obi-Wan Kenobi appearing in my hallucination. I knew something was up because I had seen this film before, and Alec Guinness wasn't supposed to be in it.

I also hallucinated another scene from a Star Wars film called Revenge of the Sith. If you have seen that film, you know there is a scene where Anakin Skywalker saves Palpatine from Mace Windu.

In my hallucination, I saw the opposite of this happening.

I saw Anakin Skywalker do the right thing.

He struck down Palpatine with his lightsaber and chopped him in half.

In turn, he saved Mace Windu from Palpatine.

The best thing about this hallucination was after Anakin calmly walked into an elevator and pressed a button, the Imperial March music began to play as Anakin stood in the elevator.

My hallucinations have a mind of their own.

Most of the time, it was the sleep deprivation; sometimes, the hunger strikes, but one thing I knew for sure was that these hallucinations could occur under any circumstances.

I'm content being sane now.

I have shown that I'm lucid.

My insightfulness is on another level.

It doesn't matter if someone disagrees or agrees with assertions I make. I barely agree with myself half the time. I did see these hallucinations; it wasn't so cool after all, and I'm laying them out here for peace.

This next hallucination occurred when I was fourteen.

Sometimes hallucinating felt like God was playing a massive joke on me.

There were a few hallucinations to do with the Harry Potter franchise of films.

I can't remember what Harry Potter film it may have been, but I just saw Daniel Radcliffe and Emma Watson sitting in stone halls, on large stone blocks, kissing.

By looking back at the screen, they would check if I was watching.

It was another one of those instances where the hallucinations were staring right back at me.

They would start making out again if I just looked back long enough.

I felt uneasy watching them kiss, even if it was just a hallucination.

The only other scene from Harry Potter is where Dumbledore visits the young Voldemort in an orphanage.

The scene seemed real; the only difference was that I saw another young actor as Voldemort.

It was much more convincing than the real Voldemort, but it wasn't. It was just a hallucination.

It is hard to explain when the memory is foggy with this one. I remember hallucinating while reading the book Prisoner of Azkaban when I was ten.

My dad had bought me the book, and I was scared because the whole book seemed to be just a vast, weird monologue seemingly written by a fictional Voldemort.

I'm not much of a Harry Potter fan, but I recognize the books as pretty good, and I did want to get around to reading them more in-depth again at some point in my life, but I don't always have time for fiction.

That wasn't the only time I experienced words changing in books, talking to me as if the text itself was alive and able to comment on me.

I can't remember what I read when I hallucinated in the form of the book Prisoner of Azkaban.

Have you ever seen The Family Man? When I rewatched this film later in my life, I was almost disappointed to realize that I had hallucinated what I had seen previously. I was disappointed.

Not only do my dreams create immersive worlds right off the cuff, but my hallucinations are also unbelievable. I found them so intriguing that I could write this book about them despite being hallucinations.

If you want my honest opinion, there are great professions, promising career choices, and fantastic workers worldwide. Actors and singers are quite simply part of that.

Some of the most remarkable men and women work in security agencies, military foundations, secret services, and even police officers, civil servants, and soldiers.

I say it without knowing too much about that line of life. I know at least where I'm coming from on an intuitive basis.

My life feels better when I write about it. Sometimes it can suck to have a mental health problem.

That can be the reality, but I'm confident it doesn't have to be that way anymore.

Instead of the actual The Family Man film with Nicolas Cage, I saw a movie where the same character starts off as someone working in a construction yard.

I saw a movie where Nicolas Cage seemed to have dissociative identity disorder.

Still, the way the hallucination of the film portrayed this: somehow Nicolas Cage's different versions of his personality split into the real world, and he had physically multiplied different versions of himself, like clones, and he was hiding all his clones inside an extensive work shed in his garden.

He was trying to organize his different body doubles in the shed, but they all had different personalities and different quirks and seemed to argue with each other, but essentially they all, in unison, looked precisely like each other, except for their demeanours in their personality, or for instance, the way they might have stood or changed the expression on their face.

That's all I remember about this hallucination film. It was great, though, even though it was a hallucination, it didn't really take away from how cool any of these early visual films came across. I hallucinated a few other aspects of Nicolas Cage from other films, so I'll mention them here too. Quite simply, I went through a phase of watching a movie like Ghost Rider. But instead, due to my hallucination problem, I would just see Nicolas Cage die in the film at the start. And then, as his ghost walked around in the movie, he would start a monologue that seemed to speak to me, and I did not know what to make. I have to admit I handled my own hallucinations well. It affected my

mental health as a young man, but I wish I had someone back then to talk to about these things.
 The Nicolas Cage hallucination would explain that he died and seemed to say something like, "Oh no, look, I've died again." But no, I do not recall what he said at all. If I were put in a lab and left to hallucinate like this, it wouldn't be unthinkable to write what is going on. I can analyze my own hallucinations to the best of my abilities. It seems the hallucinations also try to present themselves as something extraordinary. They are not, though. I assumed Nicolas Cage was the father of the kid in Jack Frost. The thing is, though, he died in a car crash at the start of the film. In the actual movie Jack Frost, which I viewed again in my adulthood, I'm pretty sure Kiefer Sutherland is already dead in the film at the start and then comes back as a Snowman. What I mean is there is no car crash to see. This brings me to two further points to do with hallucinations.
 Apart from The Multiplying Man, it seems every time in the past when I hallucinated a character played by Nicolas Cage, he would always just die right at the start. I'm sick of the hallucinations. I know how my brain used to interpret this media when I was younger. I called it The Kalvin Klein Conspiracy. I was an incredibly naive young man who simply didn't realize that no one saw the videos where people were in the same situations dying for real, or at least I thought that was how it appeared to me, suggestively. I know that sounds insane, but that is my mental health and hallucination problems. What a strange mental health problem, where I've been in my own lockdown for most of my life. The hallucinations came across as beautiful but with that disturbing aftereffect of not being real. The hallucinations seemed to possess an aura that wanted to be believed in. I was always left thinking there must be another explanation than a hallucination.
 I thought what I was seeing was technological. When I was a kid, I could go on YouTube and watch

a scene where an actress like Mena Suvari would sit around in a car and appear as though I could be seen while watching. The point is I can acknowledge that they are mental health-related hallucinations. I found them convincing. It was like the graphics got kicked up a notch as I watched. It was unbelievable to see, and the suggestion in my mind was that I thought I saw futuristic technology. It's almost like those hallucinations were trying to come across a way. You would have to experience this to know how bad hallucinating is. They are just hallucinations, but it doesn't mean that the hallucinations aren't trying to show themselves in a particular fashion.

My unwell explanation was that it is a parallel universe that was sending me out the technology. I just thought something was going on. I pondered these things about technology without knowing too much about that side of life.

CHAPTER 7
BEAUTIFUL HALLUCINATIONS

I SAW THE actress Mena Suvari in the movie Nowhere. She was sitting in a car and just looked straight into the camera, right back at me. I knew it was a hallucination, but it made me feel strange and weird.

This actress was pretty young in the film Nowhere, but the Mena Suvari I saw was closer to her current age.

So it would have been around the 2008 period when I saw this hallucination.

I also saw Alanis Morissette in the movie Dogma in the form of a hallucination. This time, though, unlike the Mena Suvari hallucination, it wasn't just a staring contest from the nether world of on-screen hallucinations.

All I saw in Dogma was Alanis Morissette towards the end, kneeling near the character Loki, who was dead on the side of the road, and she placed her hands on him. Alanis Morissette plays God in this film, but in my hallucination, I saw her heal Loki's body with her hands. Loki is an angel played by Matt Damon.

She brought him back to life.

I'm pretty sure this doesn't happen in the usual course of the film.

This was one of those hallucinations that occurred again in 2019, at the height of my illness. However, I saw this exact same hallucination when I was about sixteen.

Sometimes, like with Hell on Earth: 666, the hallucinations take on different forms of themselves, or like with this one, the Dogma hallucination, they repeat themselves at other times in my life.

I remember telling the mental health team about this hallucination.

One of the mental health professionals commented that my hallucinations are kind of like extras or deleted scenes.

The only difference is that I'm the only one who can see them, and they have no basis in reality.

The mental health professionals were pleased I wasn't hallucinating anything horrible.

I can only imagine what some people must go through.

In the film Dogma, Loki dies towards the end but is not brought back to life by Alanis Morissette.

Shortly after this Dogma hallucination, I also saw a hallucination related to the film Johnny English.

In the movie, Johnny English encounters a fake Archbishop of Canterbury, and he sees them putting a face mask just like the archbishop's on some other guy.

Johnny English also sees a man who has the words *Look busy and act accordingly, Jesus is coming* tattooed on him.

So, this leads to a scene when the French guy is trying to be knighted King, where Johnny English challenges the fake archbishop to remove the face mask from him.

It was a very convincing phony mask, but at the same time, it was a hallucination. It was the hallucination that was convincing.

These hallucinations lied to me for so long.

Nowadays, my mental health has improved, and the hallucinations have gone away for the most part.

I want to share all my hallucinatory experiences because it was difficult for me.

There were even more hallucinations in my youth, but the ones that I have mentioned are the main ones that have stayed fresh in my mind.

As a young adult, I had forgotten about the hallucinations. I had put them to bed.

Slowly, they crept back up on me, though.

The problem with these hallucinations is that they can affect the mind.

I don't particularly appreciate being sold anything, especially when it's seemingly trying to help me realize that I must become a better person and learn my faults. I prefer myself the way I am, and my mental health is good.

So back in my youth, I had a vivid hallucination.

Whenever there was a half-term break, that was usually the time during my school years when I would try to stay awake continuously. I had attempted to stay awake in the past and still go to school, but this never worked out well. If you go without sleep for long enough, your reactions get slowed down, similar to how reactions slow down when you drink alcohol a lot. I must have been either fifteen or sixteen. Those years were the culmination of my hallucinations. I thought I had discovered something. I was crazy.

The only actor I recognized from the film was Bruce Willis, and it was set in roughly 2054. I was so crazy that I thought time travel had become available on the internet. I'm well. I understand my mental health problem fine now. I, like others, can be affected easily by moving images on the screen, regardless of all the people behind those scenes.

In the movie, Bruce Willis plays an actor who suddenly finds himself on a real spaceship, and he is in the role of a captain. He is challenged to fly the spacecraft. I remember this part of the hallucination just fine. A supreme look came over Bruce Willis's face as the cinematic music played, just as he realized he would have to take control of the spaceship. The music from my hallucination was outstanding. Even as I continued the hallucination, I would listen to the music on my MP3 player. The annoying thing is, I can only remember that the music was so good. I can't remember what the damn music was at all. Knowing that would be awesome. If I knew that, I could recreate it or, at the very least, listen to it in spirit.

This is how crazy music had made me. I have nothing to lose. I found the whole Galaxy Quest remake very strange and intriguing. It's as if my mind was trying to tell me something. I'm not sure what it meant, but it was an exciting experience.

Bruce Willis landed the spaceship on a planet, and there were other actors and actresses with him, but I did not recognize them from anything else. The earth was a sandy orange terrain you would imagine somewhere like Mars. They had to fight some alien creatures and, unfortunately, most of the other actors died. In the end, only Bruce Willis survived. I should try drawing the aliens, but I'm not the greatest artist. It's almost impossible for me to describe what those viciously animalistic aliens looked like. They were like alien predators and were not humanoid, nor did they look capable of speech. It might be helpful to describe one unknown that looked like a massive bright orange tarantula, but even that is misleading. It looked more like an alien predator animal in its own right rather than something to be compared to a tarantula.

But the movie didn't have an end. It just kept going and going. The music was engaging. I was so engaged in the film that I almost forgot I was hallucinating. It was like I was there, watching it unfold, but the thing was, I knew I was hallucinating. I knew that what I was seeing wasn't real.

As a kid, I hallucinated Maynard James Keenan from Tool shouting at me as I watched interviews on YouTube. I was scared out of my life from this hallucination. I don't want to end up at a point in my life where the hallucinations are bigger than me, and then I would be sitting around watching them. I have things to do, and maybe I should allow myself to have a life for once.

The hallucinations are strange. When I hallucinate, it has been by mistake and something that I do not have much control over. There are always more hallucinations from my youth. It was a crazy time. The Kalvin Klein Conspiracy popped up again in a different version of the film Fun with Dick and Jane. By a different version, I mean hallucination. Yeah, so the final hallucination I want to convey from this adolescent period is the one of Brad Pitt and The Invisible Man. I always imagined talking about these mental health hallucinations would be dreadful. I told myself not to do it. I reasoned that it would be embarrassing. Now I can't see why I thought that. Once you get past the problem, where people think you are joking or making things up, and once they can see your close relatives and people involved with your mental health, understand how real it all comes across, then there is nothing to worry about in terms of writing about these hallucinations.

The reason I wanted to mention The Invisible Man was that it included my dad again, and what a great hallucinatory role it was. The film was set in a country like you see in Lawrence of Arabia or Ben Hur. My dad played The Magician in the film. I don't know who Brad Pitt was playing. Jesus, maybe? So my dad puts this magical blanket over Brad Pitt, and when he removes it, whatever character he was playing becomes invisible. The rest of the film was Brad Pitt running around trying to cover himself in tape and stuff like that, wearing a big disguise so that he didn't have to be invisible. I'm not quite sure what the hallucinatory film was saying. A sequel to the film returned in hallucinatory fashion one day when I stayed home from school. It was a horror movie, but you didn't find out it was a sequel until the end. There had been killings in the hotel, in a specific room, like room 27. The hotel actually became famous for it. The room was quartered off, but people still snuck up there sometimes. In the end, it was revealed to be The Invisible Man who was killing people. I think my dad should have got an Oscar for his role in my hallucination, and I mean that.

All I remember was watching a television show called Episodes with Matt Le Blanc. In the first episode, he bumped into Brad Pitt in Fight Club clothing and said, "Hey." Weird, but it was just a hallucination. He was wearing a similar outfit to at the end of the scenes in Fight Club: a bright vest and fur coat, with sunglasses. I wanted to show the nature of the unwell thoughts. I wanted to let people know how painful it is to go through.

I saw this one when it came out at the cinema. I guess people didn't see what I saw. I just saw Harvey Dent screaming his head off at the end of The Dark Knight, but it just went too far compared to the actual footage. I used to think I hallucinated that I could read Chuck Palahniuk's original copy of Diary of an Insomniac living in New York. I thought I saw the quote: *Ozymandias, King of Kings. Look upon me and despair.* The name of that book is an unreleased manuscript on which Fight Club was based upon.

There is a big difference between something called the Mandela Effect and hallucinations. The Mandela Effect is when someone misremembers something. My heart goes out to people who have hallucinated for real. If I'm aware of the hallucinations, then I won't experience them anymore. I think The Truman Show's hallucinations were the worst. The Mena Suvari hallucinations were pretty bad too. I have to forget about them and move on.

Sometimes I don't think they are hallucinations. The thing is, though, they are until otherwise speculated. All I mean is it is unlikely I will get back what I saw and show it to people. You never know though. I'm hoping for artificial intelligence to explode and shed light on the world. Well, the truth is, I think you don't really know, but it's important for me to be honest about how I think and feel about it all.

CHAPTER 8
THE HALLUCINATIONS RETURN

SO YES, I experienced a hallucination when I saw the film 12 Monkeys. This happened in 2011, after I left the hospital when I was eighteen. I was on medication at the time, and the hospital doctors had put me on a Community Treatment Order—which is just a fancy way of saying if someone doesn't take their medication, they can be recalled to the hospital legally. I wasn't sure if I had seen it before or not, but I soon realized that I was experiencing a hallucination. I wasn't entirely sure what was going on, but I didn't know what I saw wasn't real. I thought there was a grand spectacular conspiracy to it all. What intrigued me the most was that I thought my dad could see it too, but he denied that he could.

In the film 12 Monkeys, in the end, the police shoot James Cole, who is a time traveller played by Bruce Willis. In my hallucination, the younger version of James Cole appeared and shot his future self.

It was as if the boy actor had been given a spray tan and had blond hair dyed. There was a cinematic light emanating from him. To confirm, the younger version of James Cole is usually in the airport at specific points in the scenes of the usual film. However, he by no means appears with a gun and certainly doesn't change his appearance so that he is blond and tanned.

This was the return of the hallucinations for me.

In a way, the hallucinations of my youth were a big deal for me. The adulthood drama was less so, like I had been slowed down by getting well and taking medication. I never really think medication removes the hallucinations. I hope you understand, but it does usually take a bit of effort from me to go looking for them in the way I do. I thought I had discovered something in my youth. I never thought people were trying to shut me up. I just didn't want to share my experiences with the world too much back then. It took a long time for it to occur to me to write about all this. The hallucinations were life-affirming in the sense that it felt like there was something much bigger going on behind the scenes of everyday life. A brave new world? A world of pure vivid imagination.

The 12 Monkeys hallucinations would return in 2016, but first, there were a lot more hospital dramas to go through and a few more hallucinations on the way as well. I wouldn't really write too much about the hospital in a book right now. Even drawing upon the hospital in fictional stories for me is limited as well. The thing is, the hospital has been fairly traumatic for me, if I'm honest. It's not all been bad, but a lot of the experience was negative, and I think most psychiatrists understand in the sense that a patient like me doesn't want to return there anytime soon. So we have medication. An agreement is made. I take the medication, I toe the line, and I stay in the community, with all the rest of the sane, happy people.

I also saw Alanis Morissette in the movie Dogma in the form of a hallucination. This time, though, unlike the Mena Suvari hallucination, it wasn't just a staring contest from the netherworld of the on-screen hallucinations.

I saw Alanis Morissette in the Dogma healing hands hallucination scene again.

This was one of those hallucinations that occurred first in my youth and then again in 2019, at the height of my illness. However, I saw this exact same hallucination when I was about sixteen. Sometimes, like with Hell on Earth: 666, the hallucinations take on different forms of themselves, or like with this one, the Dogma hallucination, they repeat themselves at other times in my life.

I remember telling the mental health team about this hallucination. One of the mental health professionals commented that my hallucinations are kind of like extras or deleted scenes. The only difference is that I'm the only one who can see them, and they have no basis in reality. I think the mental health professionals were just pleased I wasn't hallucinating anything bothersome. I can only imagine what some people must go through.

In the film Dogma, Loki dies towards the end but is not brought back to life by Alanis Morissette. You can picture me there, watching the movie again, trying to find the scene I previously saw.

Nowadays, my mental health has improved, and the hallucinations have gone away for the most part. I want to share all my hallucinatory experiences because it was difficult for me.

There were even more hallucinations in my youth, but the ones that I have mentioned are the main ones that have stayed fresh in my mind. As a young adult, I had forgotten about the hallucinations. I had put them to bed. Slowly, they crept back up on me, though.

Hallucinating Mena Suvari and Alanis Morissette were pretty weird, but nothing compared to the hallucinations when they occurred away from the screen in real life. It was hard to confirm what was going on. I still see them sometimes in my dreams, but I'm doing better now.

In the summer of 2016, I was detained under section again and spent the next couple of months trying to get out of the hospital on a CTO.

Not long before this happened, though, I received a message on my computer from a hacker. The message seemed to be in relation to the obscure website I mentioned before and was written in the same chaotic manner of that text. The one the A&E doctor called *the mental health matrix*. When I received the message, it was during a time I was off the psychotropic drugs, and I had stayed awake for weeks on end. Unlike the Twelve Monkeys factor, though, I was able to save the message to my computer, and perhaps it was just a coincidence on the occasion, given the fact I had stayed awake for so long.

This seemed to help retreat back to my bed to sleep because I thought, well, I've got a message from the website now, I can relax.

I had the film called The Departed on in the background. I had purposely turned off the screen to leave only the sound blaring from the speaker connected to the laptop.

In the corner of my father's living room is another computer, and as I approach it, I realize someone has written a Word document on it. A hacker had logged into my computer, typed an MS Word document, and left it there for me to read. It was written in the same unique style that the author of the website used:

You delete information about you. Apology – you have nothing to be sorry for.
You owe them no explanations. They still have the information due to the reality of the Backstage and their operation centres. The act is symbolic and of some significance. You limit their capacity in the stage world. You face your so-called fear head-on and overcome it. You subliminally/subconsciously tell them you are the owner of your life and the master of your destiny.
Hospital – Assessment. Exam. Judgment. Medication. Sick Person. False impediment.
Accusing you of accusing them. When did I? I'm just mentalizing my archetypes. I said nothing to them directly to accuse them of what they are actually doing anyway. Innocent Until Proven Guilty. Spanish Inquisition. They are phantoms. Gawking in. ----------------------------

I didn't know what information I was meant to delete. Perhaps my Facebook account? But I needed that to stay in touch with people. I was just happy I received a message from whoever this was. When I showed the message to Dr Summers, he said it must be upsetting to receive messages like this and that I should not save passwords to my computer, which isn't how they hacked me, by the way. He obviously doesn't see the cool side of this.

Someone reached out to me.

In the message, it seemed they were trying to prevent me from going into the hospital too.

This wasn't really the only time I received a message in line with the website.

This never happened during my youth, only since my adulthood and since I came across the strange website.

I'm at my basement condo, and it is about 2015. I had made a point of reading the entire website in almost one sitting. This was in the first message I had received, and it happened directly on one of the archives. As I scrolled down, I read a part of the text that says "I'll give you a hint here, it's not the cute one," and at the time, I was thinking of a particular cute lady. This is because the text of the website is always telling you about true love and about a special person who you are supposed to be in love with, or falling deeply for.

I've read the website a thousand times. Such written words are not usually there. I didn't notice at the time because I just thought it was part of the usual text. I didn't know it was written there for me at that specific time.

The next time I am listening to an album called SHADY XV, and on the YouTube video, someone is typing in text, talking to me. I have stayed awake for four days, and I haven't been on medication for a while, and this is what I get, messages from the unknown hackers on YouTube. The person is just saying things like "Yeah, that's the thing about the website," and random comments like "Yeah, just say 'good' then," and just say then, "Well! You know!" there isn't much to say about this occasion, but someone was contacting me, by hacking my phone, and it's hard to remember everything the person said, but it was like they were reading my thoughts and responding accordingly.

The last two messages I received also came on YouTube.

I'm listening to a song on YouTube, and the words appear, "It's really hard to find someone who is into this…" I've checked back on the music video, and even with the subtitles on, the message isn't there. Now I'm thinking to myself, wait, is the website something to be into, like that? Well, at least I have the message from the hacker as some validation of this in my mind. The last message my father saw too and happened earlier this year in 2019, just before the hospital, really.

He was upstairs, so I called him down because on the YouTube homepage, on the search box, a further box coming off it had emerged, and the top left of the box it said insert.

In the box, someone was typing messages, but like my dad noticed, they didn't seem to make too much sense. They were coming out too fast, and the language seemed to be broken. At one point, it said, "Kundalini is up". Kundalini is talked about a lot on the website. It's what the author calls the spirit of energy. You may have heard of it from a yoga class or some tantric Buddhism book you read. I don't remember the full contents of the message, but the part I do is interesting because it says, "Go to the flat and pick up two guitars."

How did this person know I owned two guitars at my flat? But on the occasion, I saved the message from the hacker on the MS Word document; that wasn't really the end of it. This is where you can see me hallucinating Hollywood because it was like the actors from the Departed were talking to me through the speaker, live in my living room. Like I said before, the screen was just black because I switched it off, but I could still hear the scenes from the movie from the loudspeaker.

Towards the end of the movie, I noticed they were saying things that weren't part of the usual scene. There is a ray of gunshots, and then I hear Jack Nicholson say in the voice of Costello, "He shot me," but this doesn't happen in the movie. He just gets shot and dies, and it is by a single bullet, not a spray of fire. I hear the loud sound of footsteps in the snow, then I hear Leonardo DiCaprio say, "You don't do what I do." Finally, I hear Matt Damon say, "I can get you out," but it's hard to say what any of this was in relation to. I also heard Damon say, "I repeat, Sergeant Sullivan and Agent Costello are down," and after staying awake for so long, it was like these actors were speaking to me in my living room.

I don't know how to make sense of this, but it felt real at the time. It happened soon after I noticed the document appear on the computer in the corner of the living room. You don't really believe these actual men spoke to you in your living room. The truth is you don't know what to make of it. These things just happen, then you fall asleep, and life goes on. The cycle of hospital continues, and you know no one will fully understand what you experienced.

This is what hearing voices can be like. It can come in the form of technology and media devices. The hallucinations were hallucinations. The messages seemed to be coming from a real hacker, though. I talked to my psychiatrist about it, and he only seemed to see it as a negative, stressful thing for me. I liked it, though. Whoever was doing this had chutzpah. Whenever I tried to talk to anyone about it, they said I should change my password and check my accounts. It was never like that, though. I dunno, man, funny damn world.

Not long after I received the message from the hacker on the computer at my father's house, I was detained in the hospital again. There are other things too, stranger happenings, weird, wonderful, and abstract matter come to life, and I am at loggerheads in an attempt to describe myself in relation to this source material I have seen.

In two thousand and seventeen, I saw split scenes in the films Johnny Suede, The Sixth Sense, and The Whole Nine Yards. The movies I was watching were skipping ahead of each other and playing scenes in different orders, and sometimes strange things were happening in front of my very eyes. Even in Johnny Suede, I saw a deleted scene where the short midget stabs Brad Pitt's character in the stomach. As I watched it carefully, trying to screenshot this as it happened, I saw the screen taken over by blue, dazzling, shining suede shoes. You could see them dancing on the surface as they took up the entire screen. I thought of Elvis. It's interesting because I wasn't watching any deleted scenes, and I'm pretty sure these big blue shoes aren't actually in the motion picture. I could be wrong, though, or it could be another aspect of the conspiracy emerging once again.

The Sixth Sense movie was about three times as short when I saw it. Bruce Willis was saying something about wiretapping. I kept on seeing him fall down from the ceiling in a bird's-eye view type of way, like he was falling from the sky or heaven, onto his bed, and then the movie just continued. As things got worse and the situation began to escalate, I saw these weird, humanoid-robot people on YouTube with cameras going backwards to each other, getting arrested, trying to pretend they were real people, much to their robot-pain and annoyance. I didn't like the people pretending to be human on YouTube. It was at first a little bit disturbing to see this happen on the screen, but fascinating at the same time. Once again, I was going through one of my sleepless periods. This time, it was only the fourth day. Soon I would be back in the hospital, but before then, I would see this strange hallucination. My dad was watching a cop show on YouTube called Road Wars. I noticed he left the show running in the background when he went to bed. I smoked and drank coffee, peacefully happy that I wasn't on any psychiatric medication for a brief moment. I didn't pay attention to the YouTube video in the background until about three in the morning when I noticed something odd.

The first thing I noticed was that the video quality seemed poor. I saw that the YouTube video title still signified it was a Road Wars episode. Yet it wasn't at all. Instead, all it was people who seemed to be passing cheap camera phones to each other in a backwards motion sort of way. When I stared at the YouTube video, it would eventually stop on a person in the camera's view. Each person seemed to be in great distress. Their eyes were welling with water, but they could not cry fully.

These people in the grainy footage only moved backwards. One of them wore black sunglasses, though, and this person darted off into the front and then out of the camera's view. Whoever that was, he was an exception to the rule. Well, it doesn't matter because it was an unreal hallucination. I watched this weird video on YouTube at three o'clock in the morning. The footage changed to footage of two bald guys talking on microphones backstage in a stadium. Every time the view zoomed out, a flashing sign would come up on the screen: "COP! COP! COP!"

I saw things on YouTube. That's what I get for trying to stay up late.

When I was in Ashdown in 2016, I watched the film "Meet Joe Black" as they had that on DVD, and as I watched this, he was clearly wearing the lovely blue suit as he talked to Hopkins's character at the start of the film. When I buffered the film on my computer, he wasn't wearing it anymore, just the green pale suit in the rest of the movie, and then at other parts, the black bow tie event. There was a scene in the hospital where I was drying myself off with a white blanket after a shower, and as I looked at the screen, Pitt was staring back at me in this shoddy scene, holding up some white linen too. It was like déjà vu, man.

Sometimes you don't eat, and sometimes you don't sleep, and sometimes you try other things to get this so-called Kalvin Klein Conspiracy to step into gear. Other times, you see something out of the blue in totally ordinary situations. Like that time I saw a fake movie advertised on the internet, or was it fake though, or now just hidden from plain sight?

Or that time they changed the phrase from the Adam Sandler movie, a subtle and yet seemingly insignificant occurrence, but one that struck a chord with me.

Two thousand and twelve again and it's been several slow weeks just fresh out of the hospital process. I got up and I was browsing the internet on my computer for some films in the morning while

I drank a cup of coffee. I stumbled across what seemed to be a newspaper article on the internet about a Lars Von Trier film. Ones like the Telegraph, the Guardian, or even the Daily Mail.

Lars Von Trier, you may remember, from making such psychological thrillers such as Dogville or Antichrist. Either way, this film they were purporting that had been released from him is nowhere to be found, just a couple of minutes after I first viewed this article.

It was called "Nina," and I have little clue what the film was about, but from the cover, I could guess. Lars Von Trier had made a film about a fifteen-year-old German girl called Nina, and on the cover of the film displayed a young German girl with blond hair and wearing nothing to cover her voluptuous breasts, which were quite large for her age, or whatever age the actor actually was in real life.

It's weird what the psyche brings forth when you're trying to drink caffeine in the morning, but pretty soon I put this down to the Conspiracy and just moved on. By now, I was used to my mind playing tricks on me and the computer displaying vivid hallucinations. It happened from time to time and still does when I'm careful.

In two thousand and eighteen, I was watching Funny People with Adam Sandler and Eminem. In the film, Iris says to George Simmons, "I'm just going out to buy some cigarettes," and George replies that he didn't know Iris smoked, so Iris tells him she always smoked, he just didn't do it when George had the illness, but he was better now.

Simmons then says, "Just don't do it around the kids," or does he?

I was sure he said this the first time I watched the film. I know you'll probably say I'm just imagining things or getting scenes mixed up, but I'm one hundred percent sure the second time I viewed this, he says something different. Instead of "Hurry up and just don't do it around the kids," it changes to "Hurry up cause I'm kind of running out of steam with the kids." This is my life, and I watch out for things like this in the

Conspiracy. I think I missed something today. I was watching South Park online, and when I was going to the episodes, some other old-fashioned film kept playing. I just clicked off it until it worked again, but looking back, that looked like a black and white movie with a guy in it that had colour instead of everything else, which was just grayscale. I don't know, it could have just been a malfunction on the website, and the page was displaying momentarily, another movie.

  I've seen the old Obi-Wan Kenobi hunched over like a Tibetan Buddhist in robes, coming from the desert, and saying, "The force is strong with this one," except I saw him saying this to the young Anakin Skywalker in the Phantom of the Menace. How did my brain make that one possible? That was Obi-Wan Kenobi from the old Star Wars walking about in the new one, the old guy from A New Hope.

CHAPTER 9
THE HALLUCINATIONS CONTINUE

I HEARD THEM say certain strange things on the audio tracks on a feature called Zappin on my MP3 player. In Bristol, I uploaded one song from the Eminem album I had on my computer in the space I had of thirty minutes.

Zappin worked like this on a thirty-pound Sony MP3 player. There was short Zappin and long Zappin that you alternate between. Both played a small few lines randomly from one of your audio tracks on the album, at different rates due to the long and short durations. The computerized sound of a female voice would say, *Zappin in* or *Zappin Out*.

When I checked the MP3 player that night in Bristol, I had all of The Eminem Show on disk for some reason, even though I had only uploaded one track.

The next day in the courtyard where patients smoked during the day, monitored heavily by staff and tall fences, and closed at certain intervals during the day and at night time, I was listening to The Lumineers on my MP3 player. There was a lady who worked there with long braids coming from her hair, standing with the other patients by the stone bench in the middle of the courtyard. The Zappin shorted out, and I heard the voice of a Lumineers singer on my MP3 player say, "It's Juliet!"... "It's Juliet" wasn't part of any of their tracks.

Later on, I went over to speak to "Juliet" and told her about the little kid I saw on the alternative scene of young Voldemort in the latter Harry Potter movies, where Dumbledore goes to see him in the orphanage. She agreed with me, saying, "Yeah, I saw that version too. The one with the little boy in it." She called me the FBI guy because I had a cap that said FBI in bold, white cursive. Well, I don't wear it anymore, but technically I only wear whatever clothes in the hospital, depending on what is brought in for me from home.

Later on, in Ashdown back in two thousand and sixteen during this stay when I still had this MP3 player, they moved me back from Bristol, you see. A lot of the time, I didn't even mean to put that Zappin feature on and just accidentally pressed it when I was sitting down. It was the pain because once Zappin was turned on, it was near impossible to turn it off without factory resetting the whole device.

I use my headphones in the hospital to try and distract myself and make the days go a bit faster. I was listening to various albums of Nine Inch Nails in Ashdown, and while in the smoking area, I heard Zappin zone out for a second. "Guess who's giving birth to a baby?" came booming from the voice of Trent Reznor (who is the artist behind NIN) in a similar sort of way when Tupac said a similar phrase in his Ghetto Gospel song.

The difference is when Trent says it, you can't find it in any of the lyrics, and it's not really part of any of his songs.

This isn't the only time I've hallucinated a message from Trent, except the first time wasn't in the hospital and wasn't during this Zappin business.

It was shortly after I was off my medication for a few months. I was in my living room, and I had just started listening to the album The Downward Spiral by Nine Inch Nails. As I heard the music, I began to shake nervously, sort of dancing electronically to the fast music.

I moved outside to the front door to have a cigarette while I chilled to the music coming from the loudspeakers in the adjacent room. Instead of the next track coming into play, though, it sounded like it was Trent Reznor announcing to an audience at a concert or some kind of gig, but I didn't have the internet on, and this wasn't something he would usually say either.

As I was standing there, smoking the damn cigarette, waiting for the track to play, he announces, "He gave up all the fame and the murder for this?"

I'm pretty sure that wasn't on The Downward Spiral. I hadn't given up any fame and murder though. I didn't say these crazy aspects of my life would make sense, just like when I heard the actors from The Departed come live into my living room. That didn't make much sense either, but how could any of this make sense? How could famous people speak live to you in your own house or through your earphones in a mental hospital?

Back in 2012, I have another story to relate to you, which abides among similar sort of anecdotes. I had heard of Kalvin Klein and Philip Matthews now, and I was determined not to eat, at least at first. I'd sit down at the cafeteria tables with everybody else, and then when they were dishing out the food, I would just wander to my bedroom or outside in the smoking lounge. Staff would come to you after a while, in a lacklustre sort of way, and ask, "You're not eating with us today, Michael?" and you would just say you already ate when you were on leave earlier.

During this time of starvation, I saw something on the television. One night, I was walking about late, and it was during the winter, so it was dark, even though it wasn't too late in the evening yet. There weren't many people on the ward, it wasn't full for starters, which was a shocker, and a lot of people had retreated to their bedrooms after dinner.

I noticed one of those BBC advertisements had come on the television in the dimly lit living room, which was central near the smoking area in Sandalwood's Applewood Ward. Now I know the BBC doesn't schedule advertisements on their broadcast, but it was one of those suave commercials, like an M&S commercial for some chocolate pudding, advertising one of the BBC's own shows.

Or at least that's what I thought it was, or what it appeared to be, with the BBC regional accent playing over the broadcast, describing the contents of what was being shown. What was being shown? A young man with short hair and in prison slacks in an institutional youth correctional facility. There were two other young but meaner kids looking at him from across the deck. They were eyeing him up, and he had dark circles underneath his eyes and a mean look about himself too, although he was lean and kind of short.

"The Insider," said the television broadcaster, "Coming to you soon," and then the screen went black as per usual, and even at the time, in the manner of The Kalvin Klein Conspiracy, I just assumed someone else or a staff member had turned the television off, not realizing at the time that I had seen anything mischievous or untoward.

If I hadn't spoken to a staff member, I might not have realized.

When I spoke to this staff member, she looked perturbed and said to me, "Michael, that television hasn't been working all week. We've had maintenance in yesterday. What did you say it was called again?"

"The Insider," I repeated. There is no such program broadcast by the BBC, not one pertaining to the boy and the voice I saw that day. It was yet another illusion, illusions that began circling when I was in my teenage years and before that, at various stages at different houses we lived in before that.

It was interesting to note, this actually happened for once, seemingly because I refused to eat for a long time. Something in my brain won't allow me to do this anymore. I know that after you go too long without eating, it just hurts. The name of the show reminded me of an old phrase that always resonated with me: What is outside you is also inside you and vice versa. You grow up, and life carries on, but that young child that you were once, well, that person still exists somewhere deep inside.

In the 2016 period before the hospital, I had stayed awake for over five days and was about to watch a YouTube video that I had brought to my dad's attention.

It was a Public Service Announcement video with Ed Norton for the Fight Club, of which there were five or six on the internet. They were designed to be shown before the movie played at the theatre and contained the actors saying not to use any mobile phones or where the exits were in the event of a fire, and some humorous anecdotes here and there.

It wasn't the usual video of him. He looked different, more vibrant, closer to the screen, and he wasn't wearing his suit. Instead, he had a thick white shirt on, tucked into his black trousers and belt. You could see behind his shirt he had a white vest on, and his cuffs were rolled up to his elbows.

He seemed to have a sly look on his face, and he looked slightly bigger than his thin self in the Fight Club montage, although he wasn't in the least bit fat and still looked like his lean and mean self. It was quick, so hard to tell, though perhaps the setting had changed behind him from a black screen into a dark basement indeed because it was too difficult to apprehend.

Instead of the usual film specialties he was going on about, this particular one, where he was telling the audience to please turn off all cell phones and a joke at the end about never letting anyone "touch you in your bathing suit area"...

He wasn't talking along these lines, though. Instead, he was looking onwards from the screen and repeating himself, "Yes sir, no sir, yes sir, no sir," but sometimes he seemed to alternate it, "Yes sir, no sir, no sir, yes sir, yes sir, yes sir, no sir, yes sir, no sir," in that sort of rhythm, a sort of random sequence of "yes sir's" and "no sir's."

It was like he could see me in the room, and these "yes sir's" and "no sir's" were being directed at me as I took a drag of my cigarette or when I stopped. That might just be my own speculation, but whatever the case, it wasn't the usual PSA video you were meant to see. My father was there too that day, and when this video comes on, he just begins to laugh.

They say, scientifically speaking, you don't need to sleep, but your brain does need to be allowed to dream. So when you do neither, the body starts to dream quite vividly in its waking time, making life a living hell.

The computer screen can become, in effect, a clever world of very detailed and intricate hallucinations. Some doctors might even query if they are even hallucinations. How could they be when other people, online or through real-life experiences, can see these things, these indescribable things too, and comment on them, and laugh at them, and say funny things about them, then completely deny it later with a natural-based description of reality?

As per usual with these online videos, after the sequence had played, the video died, and the screen on YouTube went fuzzy black and white. This always happened with The Kalvin Klein Conspiracy. But sometimes you could get them back simply by clicking on the refresh button, although I wasn't counting on it this time.

In the old days, I remember watching an interview of a younger Ed Norton close up to the screen when he kept smiling a big red smile. If I remember correctly, it was some behind-the-scenes look at the film Fight Club.

They asked him how he does the scene where he beats himself up.

He said to the camera that most of the time he just grabs himself like this, with a motion of his hands to the collar and then says, "Then I just chuck myself, no, no," he smiles again, "We use a lot of stunts and props."

I don't know if when I saw that video it was really part of "The Conspiracy," but man, it was cool, and I wish I could get it back.

In the end, though, it just feels therapeutic writing about all this. Since I left the hospital six months ago, the only thing I've seen was that video I came across when watching the cartoon or perhaps 'pictogram' that is South Park. I didn't know it was something untoward, though. Man, I wish I had just watched it.

It could have just been an error on the streaming site.

Which leads me to think, will I ever see these aspects emerge again?

But I think it is all inevitable. I think what happened before will happen again.

You can probably grasp what I mean from the adult life hallucinations slightly better than my youthful experiences because anything from youth becomes harder and harder to recollect as time goes on. I guess nothing has compared to the hallucinations of my adult life. They were crazy. Sleep deprivation was horrible and stressful and resulted in hospital time after time. I say the hallucinations were like glimmers of hope because they were to me. It would be an understatement to call them just fun. I thought I had seriously discovered a loophole in the fabric of reality.

In early 2019, shortly after I left the hospital, there was another hallucination to do with Bruce Willis. However, seeing as I pretty much ignored it, I didn't count it much as a symptom at all and just kind of carried on my way in those early days of the recovery. I'm pretty sure the hallucination of Bruce Willis was just looking right at the screen talking to me, although my concentration was still spectacularly poor at that time, and I didn't hear a word he said, apart from something to do with listening to him. By him, I mean the hallucination.

This brings up another point with Bruce Willis and the film The Sixth Sense. I saw Bruce Willis in that film just fall from above, but you couldn't know where that above was, but it must have been through a ceiling because he fell right from the top into the bed. There is nothing spookier than hallucinating scenes in The Sixth Sense. I watched the film, but for some reason, it was entirely shortened. The hallucination of Bruce Willis trying to talk to me during the movie, but the Sixth Sense hallucination was in 2017, and my concentration had practically disappeared.

The scary thing is, I remember seeing The Sixth Sense when I was younger. I'm not sure if there is a scene in the film where the young man can see Golgotha and three crucifixes on that hill, just in the distance from where he is standing on the sidewalk. I honestly don't know if that is in the film.

I doubt it, but at the same time, I doubt the other way too. That's the hallucination, I suspect, but with The Kalvin Klein Conspiracy, I would have to check the film and watch it again.

I'm so well these days I don't check things out anymore. I do like movies, though. Don't get me wrong, I've watched many movies throughout my whole life without hallucinations. They always tried to creep back in whatever way they could, though.

As a final note, I will bring up three times I encountered a Native American hallucination in the village of Wroughton. First of all, during a hunger strike in Thorney Park.

He was tall, and I could physically see him in my dad's house, and I assumed he was there to guard me. It was directly after the film I watched with my eyeballs glued to the screen, called Indian in the Cupboard.

He appeared chieftain because he had traditional Native American colours on. Think colourful feathers. I'm not sure if it was because I was so short back then, but he looked about seven feet and naturally strong. I remember this hallucination from the age of about fourteen.

I will give you this. Like some other so-called memories, I admit memory is a problem with hallucinations like the one I mentioned with the Native American. The point to take in, I genuinely believe I experienced this in the past. However, for most of this memoir, I'm not focusing on memories like this because I could write another memoir. It becomes difficult, though, when you remember signing up for the FBI as a fifteen-year-old and randomly running around in Swindon with a gun.

My dad remembers me going on about the FBI and The Kalvin Klein Conspiracy for such a long time that I have been able to mutter words.

You would not believe the whole world of hallucinations I remember concerning the FBI, where it seemed that taken over every corner of the earth and that everyone, in some shape or form, was working for the FBI. You couldn't trust anyone, least of all yourself. I can't wait to write the memoir about the FBI hallucinations. I've not looked at my medical notes in a while, but this is mentioned in my psychiatric notes because I brought it up at various points in my illness. When I realized this was alarming for nurses, I shut my little mouth about my world of the FBI. That world was rapidly falling apart when I hit my early twenties. When I was voluntarily patient around 2012 in Salisbury, my dad said I needed to drop this talk of FBI and conspiracy. His exact words were, "Or else you won't be getting your badge and uniform back."

It is fair to say my dad has a good way of handling my mental health problem and a good sense of humour. At some points, I find myself annoyed as I write this memoir. I admit these things, the stupidity of thinking about the FBI when I'm unwell. The way I understand all of it is like the Wizard of Oz. Dorothy wakes up from a dream at the end. The land of Oz, though, it's as though I've been there. I knew I recognized my dad from somewhere. Perhaps it was indeed over the rainbow. My dad is a pretty special guy and an essential person in my life. He will never know how appreciative I am of his help in this life.

I wouldn't be here without him. I would be stuck in some corner of a mental health hospital, which is the last place I want to be.

The point is he is a pretty good dad, but I never really liked the term carer. I didn't really like anything to do with mental health. A matter of perspective.

One person's nightmare is another person's dream. My dad used to work for some kind of military intelligence, to do with computers and predicting the impact of terrorist bombs on buildings, but it doesn't imply anything other than it may have been, on some level, a source for why I thought along the lines of FBI when I was a kid. Dad used a program called BombCAD. I think he was in the team of people developing that software. When 9/11 happened, everything changed because before a terrorist hadn't thought of hijacking a plane and flying into The Twin Towers.

Around 2011, I walked to Liddington Castle with a bergen full of about three stones full of supplies. My dad came and picked me up because I was knackered and had blisters all over my feet. I had walked the distance by following the Ridgeway path from my dad's house in Wroughton. So when I walked towards Barbury Castle that day, which intercepts with the Ridgeway, I didn't tell my dad that I had heard the unmistakable sound of a Native American singing traditionally, just like One Stab sings in Legends of the Fall, which by the way, in specific hallucinations, I have seen One Stab in that film sing even more so at particular points. The more you read, the less you see. This is not like boasting but admitting a particular disability of mind. I'm OK with that.

So, just before the hospital in 2019, I was playing songs on a Jukebox at a pub in Wroughton. I had put songs on like "Summer of 69," but then I heard what I thought was someone who had put on "To the Moon and Back" by Savage Garden. I had the last laugh, though, because the track just split out into what sounded like "The Legends of the Falls," and then all I could hear in the pub was the voice of One Stab singing again. Unmistakable. Frantically, I was tapping my phone to record what was happening.

Moments later, when I looked back at the video I had recorded, it was just a few short seconds, just me walking around the pub with the camera on the view of the pub. There was no music. Goes to show you can't record a hallucination. At the time, I just reasoned I must have just recorded it wrong. I was unwilling to accept I was hallucinating. Do you want to know my thought

process before that hallucination occurred? I can't remember why I was thinking this, but this gives a rough idea:
Sometimes after the *Summer of 69*, they play *Legends of the Fall*.
So the question is, assuming *Summer of 69* literally means *Summer of 69* by Bryan Adams, 1) who are they? and 2) what do I mean by play?
So by *they*, I meant artificial intelligence. Yes, I was unwell. By play, I simply thought that artificial intelligence would play something from *Legends of the Fall*, somehow. In my mental illness, I felt that I was just like John Connor at the bank machine, getting money out the way his mum taught him when he was younger.
My final point is that for the longest time, they had just removed a scene from the original Terminator film, where you see the older John Connor in the future with scars on his face. Interestingly, though, when Christian Bale plays John Connor in Terminator Salvation, he gets three scars similarly from a particular cybernetic organism played by Arnold Schwarzenegger.
In a way, you can't blame me. With all the media these days, all the films and significant songs, sooner or later, people will experience hallucinations and mental health-related issues to do with those films and songs. It happens every day, in my opinion. All I know is I have gotten away from it. I still like a movie, but I have escaped the hallucinations.
I'm not sure if I did. I see a hallucination of Terminator 2: Judgment with Arnold Schwarzenegger, who appeared not to have aged from the first film. I definitely saw when The Terminator is walking through the mental institution towards Sarah Conor. The only difference is they played the Terminator theme music. The drums are loud and clear. Just like Last of The Mohicans, when they were playing the Gaelic music on the violins. Pretty much through most of the scenes with any violence.
That music seemed to even play during the bridge scene of the film called Rob Roy. Music changes

may sound insignificant compared to the rest of the hallucination, but when I'm hallucinating music, my heart is beating hard and fast like a drum.

See, it is like this, with anything like The Departed auditory hallucinations, or the hallucination I just mentioned with Legends of the Fall music, it doesn't matter how unwell I was. It doesn't mean, at any point during unwellness, that my thinking cap has gone. I still didn't get it right, but consider this:

Movies I watched were sometimes 10, 15, 20 years after an actor or actress had finished that film. There is no way I'm silly enough to think Bruce Willis is talking to me in The Sixth Sense when despite what I said about Mena Suvari on the one occasion appearing at a different age, most of the time, actors like Bruce Willis and Brad Pitt weren't affected by the aging process when I watched these hallucinations because of just that word. Hallucinations.

As I said, I thought it could be artificial intelligence, but even then, I have no experience in that area. People don't need a mental health problem in the 21st Century to make elegant arguments about something like a simulation hypothesis.

In terms of the hallucinations, you could say I never get better or recover. This is partially true because the idea of the kid you once still existed as part of yourself in your psyche. The kid I was, I always believed in all of the hallucinations. My basic idea as a kid was that they were all just extra scenes. Well, in that case, then I almost give up. Instead, though, I'll just shake my head and carry on.

In all seriousness, films are a great way of understanding mental health. They're brilliant at experiencing emotions of what we might be going through. Essentially, what we can relate to. When a music artist says that the lyrics of a song mean whatever meaning people ascribe to it, they're making a standard statement that music artists make, but it can be true. It is similar to how we interpret our favourite films, primarily philosophical-ridden films like The Matrix. When you look at the recent The Matrix Resurrections, the central part of the plot is that Neo is now being treated psychiatrically.

If you go back to the original The Matrix movie, you can still imagine Agent Smith psychoanalyzing Neo just like a psychiatrist. In a way, that is precisely what he does.

I don't know how I might have come across those early assessments, but I had panic attacks. I wasn't puking in a trashcan. I was puking in the hospital when I got to the adult wards at age 18. Even up until 2016, I still threw up sometimes. I'm OK, though, I have my medication, first and foremost, and that does make everything OK.

Without it, things are awful, and back then, in the early days, I was so unwell, it was unbelievable. If you didn't know much about medication, you might have even assumed I was sometimes a bit daft.

I guess at the beginning of the illness, it was embarrassing. All that trouble of having a mental health problem can make you pretty thick-skinned, and for that, I'm grateful.

I remember when I first wrote this memoir years ago. I had written something, a short memo to myself one night and showed it to my sister. She painted me a picture to go with it.

Isn't it strange to think, by the time all this has turned on its head, we'll be standing where the roof is now, and by the time our heads hit the ceiling, the gap between and the floor will be slightly larger...

When people asked me what I meant by the obscure saying, it was really a saying that only I could understand through my perspective. I used to like Star Wars a lot.

The phrase had something to do with a hallucination on the computer, which could have been an early form of fake news, but I doubt it either way.

The hallucination was just a news article from some website about how a Stormtrooper had touched down somewhere on Earth, in America. This Stormtrooper demanded to know the whereabouts of Darth Vader.

The Matrix is similar to Star Wars in the way Luke is trying to bring back the good side of his father, just like Neo is trying to bring back Morpheus from a situation that seemed unthinkable.

Movies, novels, and immersive video games are just stories at the end of the day. Notice how stories always load as Gods in the films? They don't load as programs in Matrix or even stories, but the actual Gods like the modern Neo God. Weird to think how in The Matrix fan theories and from the video games, whole cults of people worship a person called Neo. It doesn't matter how good at martial arts you are. No need to worship the person.

So if stories are just stories, what are hallucinations then, when they split off at tangents into other stories. I think usually someone who experiences hallucinations might have done this after taking a mushroom or LSD. I'm already crazy enough. I don't need to add psychedelics to the mix to induce these hallucinations.

I don't know much about that, but from what I've read, it seems that sleep deprivation has worked similarly for me, so it's crucial I get a good night's sleep. The hallucinations are stories too. They are my subjectivity seeping into the perception of the objective world, hence why only I saw them, despite seeing them in my waking, objective life. You know Elijah's theory at the end of Unbreakable? About how the archnemesis is always the exact opposite of the superhero?

I don't worry too much about that sort of thing because, no doubt, it's a great cinematic moment with significant meaning, but my dad is OK in my book.

Most of my dad's ideas of Superman came from earlier comics he read when he was younger, long before I came along. He said something about the original Superman film being more in line with how Superman would have been. So at this point, I told him, "Oh, so you know this because you knew him personally then?" My dad's response was a simple, "Yeah." I would just like to say here, thanks, dad. You really have helped clear things up in terms of my mental health. Tell Gandalf the Wizard to stop putting red kryptonite in the tea and that's what we call insight. How insightful.

One of the last hallucinations I experienced was in 2019 when I thought I heard Eminem whispering on a track that displayed that it was a crank call, titled *Is Dr Dre White?*

The whispering was done the same way Eminem whispers loudly in his Public Service Announcements, which feature on his first two albums, The Slim Shady LP and the Marshall Mathers LP. The point is, the video still showed it was playing that crank call, so it was bizarre to experience this hallucination.

Especially when I was beginning to do better in the hospital back in 2019, this hallucination was during the hospital process, as I sat out the front entrance and smoked a cigarette. The hallucinations can attack me anytime. I'm not duly worried, though. I try not to let the hallucinations get to me.

I did see both Henry Cavill in Man of Steel and Brad Pitt in Legends of the Fall appear with ginger beards. So technically, that Man of Steel hallucination occurred in 2020, but it was such a minor one that I didn't even notice at first. I just genuinely thought he had a ginger beard in that film.

I told someone about this recently, and they said, "What? So, you see that?"

Yes. I see Henry Cavill as Superman, with his black hair, everything else is the same, but he has a ginger beard. You can see why these hallucinations made me unwell; they are beautiful in making the ill mind want to believe in what the mind saw and the desire to see even more of these nonsensical visuals and auditory hallucinations.

I see where the confusion might arise.

Someone might say to me, "So you saw Henry Cavill with a ginger beard throughout the whole film?"

No, to confirm, only in the scenes where Henry Cavill is meant to and does have a black beard. Instead, I saw a ginger beard.

The same goes for Brad Pitt in Legends of the Fall. In the scene where he is leaving Susannah, that's when he has a ginger beard. Except he didn't; it was just another hallucination of my poor brain.

Well, there you go, hallucinations of ginger beards. It doesn't get any more random than that.

In 2017, I was watching 8 Mile, and I saw a scene just off the street roads in Detroit where I heard a hallucination of Eminem saying, "One shot. One Opportunity." It was pretty special, though, got to admit, even though unreal and only seen in my experience of hallucination. There was no visual image of Eminem, just the voice. I don't know why I was worried about talking about this before.

I was listening to music on my phone in the garden area of a hospital called Hazel Unit in Bristol. This is when I saw a music video for Eminem's song *Rap God*. The footage was typical at first, but then it crashed into another video of a blonde woman sputtering. The video's title hadn't changed; that was the strange thing about it. The woman said something about meat sending a signal to your nervous system that affects your brain. I tried to refresh the video, but it returned to the original Eminem video.

This was my life, hallucinating now and again whilst being unwell, then getting sectioned into the hospital and sometimes, the hallucinations continued. I never really talked about it much because they were already treating me for a mental health condition. Therefore, the main reason was that I didn't want to worry them, and I did have hunches in the past that I would write about this one day. So even though it seemed scary to write about any of this in the beginning, I talked about it rarely and kept my super hallucinations to myself.

So, these were the prominent hallucinations that occurred during my adult life. We have addressed the main ones of my youth as well. There were always more hallucinations, but I have focused on the hallucinations that have impacted me the most.

I guess a lot of the time I was thinking these hallucinations were some mystical apparition of artificial intelligence.

I don't really know, though. I find the term hallucination becomes a bit boring point to make. It doesn't go anywhere. All it assumes is that other people can't see what I'm seeing. The hallucination I heard in Beechlydene in 2019 of Eminem was classed as a shared hallucination because another patient observed the exact same thing on my phone. I wouldn't have told them about it. I had to, though, because he said something first.

My basic interpretation of hallucinations when I was younger was a funny phrase I came up with as a kid, called "Future Internet." So you know in the simulation hypothesis, our own civilization has not reached the stage of creating big Matrix simulations like the hypothesis suggests, so we would be like an ancient simulation, which doesn't seem likely.

The idea of such a big simulation would be the idea of time travel. I guess it's not really time travel, but because it's a simulation, the notion becomes possible.

I thought the way it worked was for somehow the future to be uploaded to the internet. You would then grab a link and post it on social media. The way it worked was you were supposed to post a future music video of Eminem. That's how I imagined it would work. Even if you do post the future on social media, it wouldn't have the same effect unless it was done with something like Eminem. Okay, so maybe this isn't possible.

A guy can dream, though. If it ever was possible, then I wouldn't really know how it would work, I would just be speculating.

Is it possible to hallucinate the future?

Doubt it. Nice thought, though. If I could show people what I can see when I can see it, your view would change.

Man, if I could pull something like this off, I would just lie and say, "I flew to the future and brought back the internet with me." I do have many memories of flying for a moment or two. Ultimately that's true, though, and they were hallucinations or on some occasions, a spectacular Buzz Lightyear-like fall to the ground. When I began writing this memoir, I didn't really believe in hope. I would write things like, "Who are you to tell me to believe in hope? Am I that downtrodden?" I've grown, though. I've learnt more. I've seen the pain of this life and knowing there is hope is a comfort I do not reject. Sometimes going through a lot of shit is a good way to end up embracing hope. Maybe the Superman films made it such a big ideal. I was looking at it more from a Greek mythology perspective, where everything that came out of Pandora's Box was evil. The only thing left in the box was hope. I don't want to equate hope as another evil anymore. The small things in life give me peace and fortitude.

CHAPTER 10
BACK TO THE REAL WORLD

RECENT SCIENTIFIC STUDIES support a theory about how the brain works like a filtering mechanism. That's why you forget things. Your brain is trying to make you smarter because if you had all the information in one go, you wouldn't be able to do anything. That's why we don't remember past lives or see the electromagnetic field of vision because predators would have killed us long ago if that had been so. Or so this has all been theorized. I don't know about everybody else, but I find these lines of thought intriguing.

When I experienced these hallucinations, it was a significant symptom of my mental disorder. When manifested with these hallucinations, the mental illness is like someone wearing a VR headset, who eventually remarks to the others around him, "Oh look, my headset is broken. It gives me inappropriate images and sounds that don't correspond to this simulation. I'll get it fixed."

We don't live in virtual reality, hopefully. Although it is a beneficial way of thinking about something. It could be more complex than virtual reality as the be-all and end-all of what we discuss here. I think a lot leads down the road to maths and physics, and with programming, you have a kind of modern-day technological advancement that can be thought of as magic, depending on how you define magic. From what I understand, to prevent a universe from glitching, the only programming code that would not do this would be the perfect and immutable system of mathematics itself. Therefore, it isn't programming code at all. It can be thought of as programming code in metaphorical terms, and finally, I can rest assured from the trauma I experienced when I was about nine and watched a film called The Matrix.

That scared the hell out of me. When I was nine, I thought that was real, and I had to stop watching after the part with the rows and rows of entirely realistically looking farms of human batteries.

People who hear voices sometimes explain there isn't much they can do but ignore the voices completely. The voices may not necessarily go away. Although medication can help, it won't necessarily remove auditory hallucinations. I can strongly relate to this because I know from taking medication that it does go a great deal to help, but to assume taking medication makes my hallucinations go away is just not true.

I'm saying here that I have seen hallucinations under all circumstances, including being on medication, and if I see them again in the future, then the best thing I can do is just try and ignore them. The worst thing is becoming obsessed with hallucinations because I lived life trying to induce these hallucinations in myself, and they didn't need much encouragement. It wasn't until I fully understood the nature of my mental health problem that I could get on with my life for once and forget about hallucinations that don't matter and serve here as an interesting footnote as to what it can be like to be mentally unwell.

Recovery for me has meant getting on with things. It wasn't like I didn't know that you have to work hard to get somewhere in this life. More like I had deeply concerned psychological problems. That's an understatement. I still have this mental illness, this schizoaffective disorder, which means I'm different from most people. It wasn't that I didn't want to work. We all need the money. It was more due to serious mental problems that were exhausting me in the past. I had a false sense of education due to living in a small world when I was at school. I didn't know maths had an ontology, but that's another story for another book. The more unwell I got, the less I learnt about my mental health condition, as my mind became warped around these hallucinations of grandeur.

I'm a different person today.
I wrote this memoir to come forward with my mental health problem.
Most of the time, I have gotten along with people in the hospital quite well indeed, so whatever the case, I respect the people I met. And the thing is, often in the hospital, if there was someone who I just wasn't getting on too well with, the next thing you know, they are a complete gentleman to you when you meet them in another circumstance, like another ward or sometimes simply another day. I have been terribly unwell myself in the hospital sometimes.
It was a rare time that my admissions were extremely quick because I wasn't that unwell. Most of the time, I was a disaster and needed haloperidol to turn me around quickly. Sometimes I didn't turn around as soon as I was supposed to.
Don't get me wrong, I have written about everything in my life. One of the things I do as a writer is pick something that disturbed me in the past and write about it because, although it does not make any suitable material for a fancy-looking memoir, the therapeutic value of what I learn about myself is what being a writer is all about. Writers typically spend a lot of time on their own because it takes ages to write, research, and read everything.
This is the worst idea for a writer because writers have to spend time with many people to develop a voice in the narrative that is meant to be lonely. So the writer might typically be on their own lot, writing the books, and researching marketing, but if the writer neglects to talk to other people, ask questions, and get a feeling for the world through different experiences, then it would be harder for the writer to produce something of value.
The ideal writer for me is someone like Chuck Palahniuk. Since I read Fight Club and American Psycho when I was sixteen, I wanted to write a Magnus Opus like those two books, the latter by Bret Easton Ellis. You get what life throws at you, though. I spent some time reading fiction in

my life, but I haven't read fiction in years now. There can be a lot of power in a novel.

I would like to write more about everything in this book in the future. I'm interested in everything from politics to philosophy. I won't just write anything about those things, though, because I am highly cautious about writing about anything I'm not competently knowledgeable about. So far, I've just read about concepts and opinions a lot. I need to write more notes to formulate my book on such premises.

In the future, there may be a chance to touch upon aspects of mental health again. Of course, I'm sure The Kalvin Klein Conspiracy will be there in my words, lurking beneath the shadows.

What about all the famous people I mentioned in my memoir? Bruce Willis, Mena Suvari, and Edward Norton, to name a few. I gave an objective view of what I experienced, what I saw, and how I saw it and avoided explaining what they might mean regarding my consciousness and mind. Nevertheless, the main thing here is to remain defiantly unabashed about it. People have different opinions about the rich and famous. Without art, we would not have our favourite songs and favourite movies. So, art is essential then. Actors are highly trained actors, and music artists can appear as a genius. Music is an excellent way of freeing oneself from specific limiting points of view. You may have grown up in a strict household but been attracted to rebellious music.

With films, you have ideas. I'm an idea person myself. Books and films are the primary sources of ideas I can think of. Whatever the case, I'm left with one thought.

In the novel by Chuck Palahniuk, the fighting and the rules of Fight Club aren't important. They provide a structure, a beat, and a hook to the novel, where the author allows himself to keep the reader's interest going long enough. It sure was a suitable method of repetition and displayed a truth that many people just like lists. Initially, I planned to write this book with memoirs about the hospital drama and the hallucinations as a sort of timeline that occurred mainly between hospital admissions and sometimes, as you have seen, during the hospital admissions, such as The Inside Man hallucination.

Obviously, it didn't work out how I mentally evolved as a writer. I decided to leave other musings about mental health on the back burner and present you with this short read about the hallucinations of my schizoaffective mind. The hallucinations aren't that impressive when I just write them down as I see them. Although they were imposing to experience, they can feel stale and repetitive for me to write about.

I haven't seen any hallucinations barring that ginger beard in 2019 in a long time now. The great thing about writing the hallucinations in this memoir was they allowed me to be honest, but at the same time, that same honesty provided a pretty good structure for expressing myself as someone with a severe mental health condition.

Hopefully, I won't see the hallucinations again on the screens and audio players. Perhaps I will just know the truth of reality as I look to the stars. Of course, as a final note, my mental illness always sought ways to convince my mind of what I saw. It seems so real.

At the same time, you can see how the mind plays tricks. With The Kalvin Klein Conspiracy, I always sought an irrational explanation.

Human beings describe themselves through stories, myths, legends, religions, and anything allegorical. In the future, when the world is at peace, humanity may increasingly explain their world through mathematics, physics, and rational philosophy. I look forward to seeing you all in the new Star Trek future, when deep space exploration ramps up and humanity, as one, embarks on a new quest to explore space and time together, through the universe, forever.

I'm hoping in the future, AI will advance to a point where the technology can detect phenomena such as hallucinations and therefore help with mental health.

A question might be, how?

I don't know because I don't work in that field. I know it is a possibility because no one knows what the future might hold regarding artificial intelligence. People working in the area have different ideas about the term artificial intelligence. AI might be able to do beautiful things in the future. I don't need to have experience in anything to see AI is already making great strides in this world.

For example, AI has allowed surgeons to practice their discipline in virtual reality. Technology like that seems indispensable to the way the world is moving forward.

Despite the fact they are hallucinations, no one knows what might occur in the future. If they become detectable in the future, it doesn't necessarily mean they will not be hallucinations anymore. The human body has five senses. AI may develop even more. Sounds like science fiction. I'm sure anything will be possible on a long enough timescale with AI.

I remember thinking, *Sentient agents*. I saw it like The Matrix, where agents can take over any human body. I reasoned that they would not have to change the shape or form of the human in any way. I didn't think this was happening in real life.

It was how I explained the hallucinations to myself and remained sceptical. All I mean is that I thought a sentient agent could easily take over the pixels of the body of an actress or singer on screen and change the usual course of a scene or song.

At the very least, this was the beginning of becoming distrustful of the hallucinations. It's not in line with the truth, though. That's the problem.

The Matrix is a science fiction film. The basic idea is the same as The Terminator. AI as a superintelligence that spawns even more superintelligent versions of itself until it destroys the people who created it. I love those films, but at the same time, although there is a lot of caution about AI, I think its impact on the world is going to be magnificent and a great thing for real change.

There could be better living conditions, longer lives, and reduced crime. Maybe it's hard to see how artificial intelligence could improve someone's mental health.

AI could not replace being able to talk, share, and interact with human beings. At the same time, it could be time to learn with whatever AI a person can get their hands on.

Eminem is an admirable person to many people who listen to music. For people reading this book, imagine anyone who comes across this way for them in the media, then imagine what it would be like to experience the idea of all these hallucinations.

If anyone like me, the hallucinations are vicious because they lend to a mental health problem, where I thought there was something to it.

I think there can be something to it, either mental health on its own or even with technology, that can help with hallucinations. It doesn't change the truth that none of this was real. That doesn't change the reality that I still saw and heard it. I always felt left with questions about whether people thought I was joking, lying, or making all this up.

I think it is clear to see that I'm in no way bearing a false account. I have hallucinated and written about the hallucinations coherently. I have shown how disturbing thoughts are related as an aftereffect of hallucinating. In the midst of all this, I found a way to hope for a better way of understanding hallucinations.

I remember when Eminem used to be played on rotation on the radio. Those were the good old days. Those days may come again.

CHAPTER 11
CLARK KENT

WHEN I EXPERIENCED these hallucinations, it was a significant symptom of my mental disorder. The Matrix scared the hell out of me. When I was nine, I thought that was real, and I had to stop watching after the part with the farms of human batteries.

People who hear voices sometimes explain that there isn't much they can do but ignore the voices completely. The voices may not necessarily go away. Although medication can help, it won't necessarily remove auditory and visual hallucinations. I can strongly relate to myself because I know from taking medication that it does go a great deal to help, but to assume it makes my hallucinations go away is just not true.

As I set out to write this memoir about hallucinations, in the back of my mind, I was unaware that it would bring back the traumatic nature of it in my mind. It has not killed me, though, and I have become stronger for it. I'm saying here that I have seen hallucinations under all circumstances, including being on medication, and if I see them again in the future, then the best thing I can do is try and ignore them.

The worst thing is becoming obsessed with hallucinations because I lived life trying to induce these hallucinations in myself, and they didn't need much encouragement. It wasn't until I fully understood the nature of my mental health problem that I could get on with my life for once and forget about hallucinations that don't matter and serve here as an interesting footnote as to what it can be like to be mentally unwell.

Recovery for me has meant getting on with things. I still have this mental health problem, this schizoaffective disorder, which means I'm different from most people. I wrote this memoir to come forward with my mental health problem. Most of the time, I was a disaster and needed haloperidol to turn me around quickly. Sometimes I didn't turn around as soon as I was supposed to. In the future, there may be a chance to touch upon aspects of mental health again. Nevertheless, the main thing here is to remain defiantly unabashed about it.

Initially, I planned to write this book with memoirs about the hospital drama and the hallucinations as a sort of timeline that occurred, mainly between hospital admissions and sometimes, even during hospital admissions. It didn't work out that way. I mentally evolved as a writer. I decided to leave other musings about mental health on the back burner and present you with this read about the hallucinations of my schizoaffective mind.

The great thing about writing the hallucinations in this memoir was that they allowed me to be honest, but at the same time, that same honesty provided a pretty good structure for expressing myself as someone with a severe mental health condition. Hopefully, I won't see the hallucinations again on the screens and audio players. Of course, my mental health problem always sought ways to convince my mind of what I saw. It seemed so real. I looked at shows where people did have superpowers and asked, as a child would, "Is any of that possible in the real world?" Shows and books often show the powers and ability thing, with the roles of villains and heroes.

I'm not sure why so many hallucinations were about famous actors and, on occasion, music artists like Trent Reznor. Maybe it's because I watched many movies and listened to music too much. This has been a mental health problem, and although not something to be ashamed of, I'm not trying to make hallucinating sound cool. In that sense, I have definitely succeeded. I have never studied psychology. I've read about it, and it seems interesting.

Come to think of it, I'm not so integrated. I learn some maths at university, but I'm not living to my full potential. I want to know everything I can understand. Here are some topics of interest that make my brain tick:

- Quantum physics
- Ontological Mathematics
- Philosophy
- History
- Jungian Psychology
- Gnosticism
- Artificial Intelligence

It is intriguing how mathematics is at the forefront of everything. Reading about maths motivated me to take mathematics at university. Studying languages can be a great route because a person can speak to other people in different countries. Studying history is also essential. The subjects I previously mentioned, such as Ontological Mathematics, are subjects I am interested in. I don't actually know anything about it. I need to gain more experience. I need to get out there more. I don't know exactly how to do that. I think I do not understand the inner workings of my psychology at all.

I have something to mention about the nature of superheroes. In comic books, superheroes are always here to maintain the current order and status quo. In a way, superheroes are dead. They never die, even when they definitely die. A superhero never comes along to overthrow the current way of life. People don't want that; it's a crazy idea. The superhero never causes a revolution, God forbid revolution. Anything but revolution. Humanity's notion of what it means to be a superhero is weird. I'm left wondering why I thought I was Clark Kent. It's called a mental health problem and it isn't always pretty like Clark Kent in Kalvin Klein clothes. All those hallucinations made me think I had a remnant of x-ray vision. Of course, if I were Clark Kent, I wouldn't need to go to the gym. That's something I can get on board with. What other perks does this delusional thinking have? Clark Kent eats a lot of junk food due to boredom, but it has no impact on his body because he is an invulnerable alien who doesn't actually need to eat. Sunbathing can't hurt him and, due to the radiation, would probably give him waves of energy, like he was charging up. Clark Kent would be impervious to smoking and drinking. Any notion this would take away his powers is foolish. So everything this Clark Kent did would be an act of a pretender. He would have pain receptors that allow him to simulate agony and even injury or a cold. Smallville and Metropolis would have been swept up just like Dorothy's House in The Wizard of Oz, and the rest would be packaged and sold into a profitable entertainment business. Superman wouldn't be that muscular because he wouldn't need to be. Clark Kent's power lies in his mind, apparently, but as long as he knows he is just a fictional character, he should be no danger to the public.

To think of it, believing I was an alien was never the most innovative idea. In many ways, I never did. At the very least, though, I considered it a possibility, and then I realized this was all it came down to strength. The strength of mind is what I'm interested in most. That's great. I'll have to work on my mental health and my attitude problem. I don't need to issue a complaint to anyone. I blame myself for watching too many movies and listening to too much music. Comic book characters remain in the comic books, and I'm left with a feeling that sometimes in life, I have to recognize the lack of my intelligence. I don't think it's good to go around this life thinking I'm so bright. That's why I have never done that. Clearly, some intelligent people are out there, and part of my reasoning here is to recognize that I'm not as bright as I imagined myself, significantly when growing up. Albeit, delusions of grandiosity like this are part of the symptoms of my mental health condition. It has been a pleasure to write this memoir, as the therapeutic value is something I don't underestimate.

Movies fascinated me when I was growing up, like the film Goodfellas, where the young Henry Hill is impressed by how the gangsters park their cars on the side of the road and never get a ticket. Then I grew up, slowly but surely, and that old situation where I sat down and watched a movie was lost. I haven't sat down and watched a film properly in a long time. Everything is paused or is now Netflix on my computer, and I haven't watched a good crime film in a long time. Instead, I turned to books. Even when I was younger, a book had been produced into a film at some point. I've been reading the Pythagorean Illuminati books for a long time, but I think they don't get as much coverage because they are one of the few voices out there that will tell you what they think, despite the climate of political correctness. One of the things the books pointed out was that smartphones are more like dumbphones. There was no census by the government into how these corporation-run phones would impact our lives globally and personally. It's interesting to get these points of view from somewhere, and I wouldn't like a world where I didn't know anything. Sometimes it seems we live in a world where knowing nothing is valued the most. I don't believe we live in a Matrix. At the same time, I think the Matrix has created a fascinating hero's journey. Convert the story into a real-world scenario and figure out if your life can be as exciting as an action-packed drama on the silver screen. It will never be, and I didn't need a movie to tell me that. Indeed, I do not need virtual reality headsets to inoculate me. I live in a basement flat with mould, and it's damp. I don't need anything. Every time I wake up, my eyes are tired.

I have food and water. I never was that into computers except when I was little and I found out it could be used as a console. Now I'm older, and I'm sick of video games. So, in The Matrix, the computer programming of the neural interactive simulation is run on green Chinese letters in the form of a digital rain code. At only some point in the movie, the code is displayed as numbers. Imagine going back in history to when the learnt and the smart were at the top of the food chain in society, but of course, there never really is that essentially in a film. A film wouldn't be trying to educate me now, would it? I had enough of that at school. I don't know much about Descartes, and it's hard to see those knowledgeable people whose opinions are probably exciting. I was hoping you wouldn't take my opinion too seriously. I'm not that intelligent, nor do I have many qualifications. The intellectual ones were never at the top of the food chain, even in history, but they were easier to see from the onset of how society is built up. I wanted to catch up on intellectual thought over the last four hundred years, but it is not as easy as it sounds. I still want to learn more about the nature of history. I can learn about humanity's early reasonings in philosophy and politics. Studying ancient Greek civilization is essential because the modern world's scientific and technological advancement is undoubtedly indebted to those Greeks. So with Nietzsche's Superman, he was interested in how future people might be more mentally and cognitively advanced. With Superman, you have someone with advanced physical prowess. You could argue that both come down to the same process of mind power, but then, in my opinion, this doesn't lead to meditating underneath a tree to sharpen your focus. I might do well to give it a try, though. An interesting idea as I definitely don't meditate in the garden enough. It's calming for mental health. Helps me breathe. That's what I love about the winter. Big, deep breaths of fresh, clean air.

So long ago, I wrote this book. Ever since I was little, I have wanted to write. Things have changed since I came up with a phrase, The Kalvin Klein Conspiracy, and I was wrong when I was younger. I thought it sounded cool back then.

Hallucinations are a funny thing. I have learnt that hallucinations can be the most frightening thing for people. They can also appear as the most beautiful thing. Yes, they can look that way. Either way, most of us who have experienced them try to get as far away from those experiences as possible. How weird I was as a young boy to think that writing the English language would be pretty straightforward. There is nothing quite like it, the adrenaline rush of writing. Cops, criminals, extreme sports athletes; they don't know half of it. The thing is, maybe I'm just really nervous these days. There is nothing that can actually help me in that regard. My nervousness never goes too far away. When I was little, I wanted to write my book straight away. When I set about to write it, I realized I didn't know much. Not much has changed, but I've managed to get away enough from the hustle and bustle of things to write this memoir of healing. The Kalvin Klein Conspiracy was always imagined as a graphic novel. At one point, I had never seen a comic book, and it was drawings. I tried writing about it at one point, and it came out as if it was written fast so it could be sold dirt cheap. The contents were inspired by early hallucinations while playing video games. After school was out, and I had spent all those years in mental health hospitals, I wanted to write about my experiences with mental health problems. It has been a struggle. I showed my writings to my dad, and he always gave me lots of encouragement and a critical eye. Several years passed, and a lightbulb switched on in my head. Time to write about these hallucinations I've been hiding for so long.

CHAPTER 12
WHAT IS REAL?

SO, AFTER THE hospital debacle of 2019, I had to reformulate my life. I began to lift more regularly. I upped my squat to 180kg, my bench press to 130kg, and my deadlift to 200kg. It was the best thing for my mental health: to show some serious physicality and get real strong. I also studied math at university. I did well in my first year. This is what I recommend to people in similar situations to myself. Don't worry about the medication too much. Just try and get on with things, whether it be work, the gym, sport, memoir writing, or anything that inspires you. At the end of the day, mental health workers are just human beings, and a lot of them have been in the hospital too at some point, so don't worry about it.

What we do in this life really does echo in eternity. Become a hero today and let your name be remembered forever like Achilles. Conditions on earth are better than they have ever been. No one has seen what it was like for the people in the days when Rome ruled the world. There may always be great suffering in the world. Who knows? The point is that I have a flat, food, coffee, cigarettes, and an internet connection. This is unbelievably good. I never knew this would be possible. I have even gardened and learnt about technology. I respect people's decisions about wanting to die. I appreciate that sometimes there is nothing, not even the finest doctors on earth, can do.

I'm not saying heaven, the afterlife, or even that God does not exist. In all probability, those things do exist. You could still choose to survive instead. By survive, all I mean is this comes down to strength and physicality. There may be loads of factors at play, but it does not matter. Anything can be beaten with physicality and strength. Mental health is the same thing. In fitness, they call it mental fitness. In some areas, they talk of mind over matter. In other places, you might have heard "brains over brawn." It all leads back to the same thing, though: train, learn to fight, run, lift weights, work out with a purpose.

Water is vital. Get plenty of that. The caffeine in Western civilization is terrific. Perhaps you have other things to do. I will go back to training as usual. In this life, we don't know what is coming next. Times could get better or worse. Either way, I'll stick to physicality and strength. I used my strength to write this mental health memoir, and I'll use my strength to survive as usual. Quantum computers have arrived, so anything will be possible soon. There is hope. I have seen it.

I'm just some thirty-year-old from Swindon, and I thought I'd write this book to display what a mental health problem can be like. The inspiration was a younger version of myself who believed he had access to a Director's Cut of *Fun with Dick and Jane*, which kept going on forever and never finished on the screen. Well, that was some recovery. Insult mainstream psychiatry as a profession. God damn you, God. My dad isn't a fan of blasphemy. I'm not my dad, though, and I don't believe in blasphemy or God. The phrase is the ultimate expression of frustration, anguish, and madness. Well, if anything ever does surface online about the footage I have talked about, which I classified as a hallucination, I am going to look clever for writing about it in the first place. Okay, technically that hasn't happened and probably never will, right? I guess it doesn't really matter as the whole idea is vague and maybe even a little vain. The last time I was in the hospital was in 2019. I've done really well since then. I managed to start working manual labour occasionally, I managed to complete a few years at university, and I wrote like a maniac while increasing my strength at the gym with a power bar and some serious weight. One session I aimed to lift 1000lbs with just 1 rep from squat, bench and deadlift and actually managed to complete the workout. It involved a lot of careful warming up, as the weights get bigger, the reps reduce from 5 to 3 and then 2 and 1. I read a lot of guides and articles on the Stronglifts website to learn how to do all this with proper form and safety. I got my dad into the training as well, and he was proud of me when his strength increased and suddenly he could leap about again.

I value the wellness and clear head I have today. I like the life of writing, lifting, eating well, and enjoying my time with the ones I love. So yeah, Elon Musk has popularized the concept that humans live in a simulation. His basic argument is that if you look at the rate at which video games have advanced to lifelike immersive images, in about forty years going from a game called Pong, then the chances we do live in some kind of simulation. It raises interesting questions because we are currently a civilization without the power to run reality deep simulations ourselves, so then what would we be, a prehistoric world for a certain reason? Seems unlikely, but a lot could be possible if we did live in some kind of technological simulation. It's not such a crazy idea.

The reason I like it is that even if we don't, it still stands true as a great metaphor for understanding certain things, like the films *The Matrix* always show us. Who here hasn't really experienced the glitches of *The Matrix*, *The Simulation*, or *The Real World* or *The Knowable Universe?* It's the metaphor that's important. It gives you a little story model to map how you see the world.

So if we did live in a simulation, then dreams as well as hallucinations would be by-products of that simulation. Everything would be artificial. Okay, we don't live in a simulation. The dreams and hallucinations could still be artificial, just in another way, or in a similar way. See, I told you, it's good a metaphor for understandings and drawing fast conclusions. Well, I guess there is a lot more to it.

Some people called the universe a Collective Dream, made up of over seven billion dreamers on Earth, and possibly even more people out there if other regions of space, if they exist, who we call aliens. When you dream, you are alone. When you are awake, you dream together with all the other people in the world as we all consciously create this existence. Maybe that's a terrible way of putting it, but the idea is you can't fly in the real world because it's a Collective Dream with things like our current understanding of the Laws of Physics.

I'm hoping in the future AI will advance to a point where the technology can detect phenomena such as hallucinations and therefore help with mental health. A question might be, how? I don't know because I don't work in that field. I know it is a possibility because no one knows what the future might hold regarding artificial intelligence. People working in the area have different ideas about the term artificial intelligence. AI might be able to do beautiful things in the future. I don't need to have experience in anything to see AI is already making great strides in this world.

For example, AI has allowed surgeons to practice their discipline in virtual reality. Technology like that seems indispensable to the way the world is moving forward. Despite the fact that they are hallucinations, no one knows what might occur in the future. If they become detectable in the future, it doesn't necessarily mean they will not be hallucinations anymore. The human body has five senses. AI may develop even more. Sounds like science fiction. I'm sure anything will be possible on a long enough timescale with AI.

I remember thinking, *Sentient agents*. I saw it like *The Matrix*, where agents can take over any human body. I reasoned that they would not have to change the shape or form of the human in any way. I didn't think this was happening in real life.

It was how I explained the hallucinations to myself and remained sceptical. All I mean is that I thought a sentient agent could easily take over the pixels of the body of an actress or singer on screen and change the usual course of a scene or song. Okay, so maybe I'm really good at drawing incorrect conclusions, but I think it shows a great insight. I've tried my best to show you that the hallucinations are linked to the mental health problem I have. In that sense, an irrational explanation always followed the hallucinations.

Most of the hallucinations were of famous people.

Well, most of them were either Hollywood or the music industry.

Maybe my brain found a fertile ground to hallucinate because of the fantastic and sensational manner in which films and big songs come across to the public eye.

The main part of The Fun with Dick Jane Hallucination I remember was Jim Carrey sitting on a computer reading text files full of the phrase repeated continuously, "KALVIN KLEIN," as he remarked there were thousands of these documents. The ending was different. It seemed to just go on and on. I thought I had access to a Director's Cut version of Fun with Dick and Jane when it was actually my hallucinatory brain.

So what I find really helps with my mental health is to make up rhymes and attempt to learn them, because it's harder than it looks. I'm not a rapper, but I've always listened to a fair amount of hip hop, so it's really challenging and pretty much good for my mind to try and do this. I mean, I'm thirty years old, I'm not trying to join a musical or anything like that, but it's not time-consuming, it feels great to be in touch with my intuitive side. So I find the rhyming kind of worked in a similar way to my early story, *The Kalvin Klein Conspiracy*, where I was trying to shock people into listening to what I had to say.

So this is what I came up with, after basing the idea on someone called Anarkial, who was a villain character I was developing for my novel.

Yeah yeah yeah Anarkial
My name is Anarkial
Cut your head open like a car key hole
Scoop out your brain like an ice cream cone
Leave a crime scene investigation more dangerous than CSI Miami on a late night show
Return to the scene of the crime the next day saying "What happened here? Oh no!"
Taking DNA Swabs of the people I killed
Impersonating an officer for a cheap thrill
Watching the rest of the cops get suspicious
Get a yellow taxi cab out of there and give them my best wishes, screaming "Yes, those brains were delicious!"
Get out on the sidewalk. Bump into a blind man called Bob
Steal his cane from and beat him over the head with the end of the rod. Look at this poor sod. He looks like he has been trampled on by wrath of Zod
Go over to the street corner, meet a drug dealer called Wanda
Make a new order of amphetamines for my neurological disorder
Take the whole pack in less than an hour, die of an overdose, a heart attack whilst I was in the shower
Find myself in hell, in a prison cell where the only telephone calls are from phone sex gals, with a warning on the wall, saying don't eat the candy on the floor, and everytime I bash my head against the wall, I wake up in hell's hospital drinking food from a straw, spent six months in there and all

I don't know, man. I guess I don't have all the answers. Maybe it doesn't matter if people label existence as a simulation. I know I want to get back in touch with my spiritual side. I'm not sure what the full extent of that means. Meditation does seem like a good option for someone with a mental health problem. It could help clear my mind, allow me to focus, and re-energize.

I know I've been bitter in this memoir, as I've tried to cling on to the hallucinations like they could come back. It's no way to live, though. I have to move, grow, and evolve. I'm thirty now, but I feel like I still have a lot of untapped potential. The medication does help, although I'm not a psychiatrist myself and I can't tell you how all the tablets work really. I take a mood stabilizer, an antipsychotic, an antidepressant, and an anti-side effect medication.

My doctor mainly decided the medication routine for me.

I've gotten used to the combination. When I don't have it, I can lose insight pretty fast, and then when I get there, I don't really want to start taking it again until someone gets a hold of me. It is good, though. For example, in the gym, with heavy weights, you want to be level-headed and calm. So if you have a mental health problem and want to do strength training, then taking the prescribed psychiatric medication helps.

It's important to remember that mental health medication is prescribed medicine from real doctors. Psychiatrists aren't charlatans, and medical advice is meant to be taken seriously. It's unbelievable how important the psychiatric medication becomes. It's really good, you know, to be able to be stable and get on with your life. You look at all the unwell times and wonder why it had to be that way so often.

I've written so much over the past ten years or so. Before that, I always wrote from time to time, but there was a brief period in adulthood where I became unwell, and writing was almost like new to me again. It was strange, but I soon got back into the pattern of things until I found my own simple and effective voice. A lot of my novel drew upon ideas from mental health or the hallucinations. So, like with The Invisible Man, this was who the character Anarkial was based on, although he didn't rap in the book.

I came up with the name when trying to think of something that meant spirituality found in anarchy. Initially, this bad guy was just called The Bomb Man. What I want to do is release a larger memoir called 2028: LOTL and tell you all about how I see the world, what I get up to, and form a real kind of narrative that continues from this book and finds an even stronger voice.

I still want to write stories, but I have to admit, it's like a whole career that I haven't trained for properly, despite writing like a maniac each day. So with the novel, it's more like a memoir to me because it's so heavily drawn from my hallucinations and strange beliefs about the glitches, simulations, and deja vus. I think I will show it to the world.

So not all the rap rhymes were as bad as the Anarkial one. I thought I would share them in my memoir because the process of trying to articulate myself has been good for my mental health. The first one I would like to share is some rhyming about Spiderman.

Will the day that I fall you will never say that I'm not saving you
Quite simply if I am not, then I will just not be a superhero
And I just not Spiderman
Initial thoughts, when I'm a stop spinning you
Weaving villain caught in traps, spin them around and throw toxin
Woman are shocked, the comic books could not get unbreakable to rock
Mr Glass is just not on this track
I'm stealing you now, sense me or not, I'm show you like
The wrath of God was born in a cot
Bear witness a lot, cities are mocked
Is it is spectacle or I'm just a superhero or not?
Will I the day I fall I'm swinging through the city, long as you need me
Will the day that I fall, you'll never say that I'm not saving you
Therefore if I am not, then I'm a stop swinging through
Then thus I'm just not superhero, and I will be just not Spider-Man
Invisible webs, when will I stop weaving you?
Villains are caught in traps, spin you and throw toxin,
Hail the beast like rush, the hero inside cannot let up, nor the danger persist
The courage to never back down, give in? It just won't ever exist
Aunt May, Uncle Ben, Mary Jane and Venom, Green Goblin from school days, his son Harry and Gwen Stacey
My actions are strategic, I act like I'm an acrobat, I swing like I'm addicted to the thrill, no turning back
Will the day that I fall you will never say that I'm not saving you
Quite simply if I am not, then I will just not be a superhero
And I just not Spiderman

Initial thoughts, when I'm a stop spinning you
Weaving villain caught in traps, spin them around and throw toxin
Woman are shocked, the comic books could not get unbreakable to rock
Mr Glass is just not on this track
I'm stealing you now, sense me or not, I'm show you like
The wrath of God was born in a cot
Bear witness a lot, cities are mocked
Is it is spectacle or I'm just a superhero or not?
The unstoppable web-slinging, crime-fighting mad man
With minimal fear, protecting the lives of the city around
I saw you standing in town, sense me or not, I'm stealing you whether you like it or not
Just like without me the transubstantiation cannot be a shock
Bear witness to this talk, heroics that rock
Am I saving the city or am I just a by-product of mouthed off talk
My ridy on my mcbidy, so get this, gather round, you tidies forgot
Spidey does not give up!

So far I have been able to read out my own verses, but the nature of memorizing lines is something I haven't got the hang of yet. Rapping is harder than it looks.

I've always been a fan of the hip hop genre since being a young man. For me, I love the beats and the lyrics are probably the most meaningful part of the experience for me, although I mainly listen to older stuff, if I'm honest. I think with hip hop it was always big, but nowadays, hip hop is titanic in size and has seemed to dominate the music industry.

My next rhyme is about The Matrix.

Sometimes you wake up and you feel like shit
And there is nothing you can do to make that better
And that sucks
But if you could
Would you use music to elevate your spirit?
But what if it was interactive process?
So the music wouldn't be static
There would be a rhythm
So shift the perspective from listener

To creator, and watch your mood excel

Fake American Accent, I dunno, do this shit by accident

Name's Kal
Been around, since saved by the bell
Grew up in a Matrix
Escaped it
Came back
And watch their faces
As I beat the shit out of them
With one hand tying my laces
Never been greater
How's your day your been?
In this simulation
Cause I worked it later, whilst I working out earlier
Information searcher
Watched The Matrix give birth to
A generation of AI that spawned an entire race of machines
Then I watched The Matrix get lean
How you been?
It's been a while in the simulation
De Ja Vu is a certain sensation
People confuse it with love all the time
It actually means the machines just changed your mind
For all and intents purpose, I just said this shit for a dime
What you actually think I know, kung fu, karate, Tae Kwando and something drunken boxing?
That would be sick I would like Charlie Bronson
I could be a superhero just like Flash Johnson
Whoever that was, a vigilante with a stupid name that's nonsense
That's what I always wanted, to be a problem
In this system, in The Matrix Control bliss realm
Just a rogue son of a gun
With a pun in his hand about the red sun
What you need? Get some
Just run, for the hills
And scream, what a gwan
So resurrect
Alive or dead?
Just get up

Over here, gather round
And you'll see
That's it's me
A calm little bomb, round this room, so gather round, hear me now, ear to the ground, don't look up, not just yet, stay close to the floor, and what's more, you can hear, the drums of the shore, beating high and so low, hearing me, hearing yo, so let's go...Ayo

Retreat to your exits, it's meant to be
Agents are coming. Shift your perspective
Agents.
Lockdown, War in Ukraine, Coronavirus, the Simulation Hypothesis and the twenty first century
Next to be?
Agents are next. I tell you Agents are coming
I've done this before
Knock them to the floor
Smack them up
And then hit them in the core
Handle them all
With just one hand
For sure

Then these men dressed up in suits
Turned up to attack
So I snapped
And ripped both of their necks in half
For a laugh
Fighting is dancing, there is nothing quite like it
Punching and kicking, without giving ever giving a shit
So listen up, here' the bill
Blue or red
Take the pill
Come with me now if you want to be kill-DUH.
Twenty first century,
get to where your meant to be
realise humanity
has been taken over by virtual reality
Computers everywhere, subliminal networks
and a hex upon the Matrix whilst you sit at work
The machines uses intelligence to cause a glitch over us

But if you can understand the nature of the system that you think you still trust
Then I must insist here, it matters not whether it's symbolic, real or allegory
The Hero's Journey written is in code with in a Godlike story
Fighting sentient agents like a rebel rogue mercenary

```
To be clear, I'm not really trying to be a rapper.
It's just something I do from time to time, to
help with my confidence and because I enjoy it. It
allows me to be creative in a different way. The
next verse I would like to share is more of a
light hearted one.
```

Hello children, what do we say to strangers?
We call them strangers, we shout strangers right to their faces
That's the way I was brought up with a strong hand
I smoke cigarettes constantly all day long
My throat is burning, I think something is wrong
Oh well, just have a really raspy voice now
That's the way the cookie crumbles I guess
And Friedrich Nietzsche said, "God is dead." But who killed him?
It was me, no it was him, no, it was wait, no wait it was, no
It was a bird, no it was a plane, hang on a minute
I think that is Ubermensch
You know what this means
I am become a monster
Death becomes him
I am become death
What doesn't kill you makes you stronger

The thought police after me but next week is hate week
The all singing all dancing big brother is around here somewhere
Watch his eyeballs move on the old painting and poster
Infiltrate the junior anti sex league for closure
The doubletalk is hard to keep up with
Home is where the heart is
And familiarity breeds contempt
But the heart only grows fonder
If only Willy Wonka was here right now
With Archie and the rest of the gang

But what about the Brady Bunch
No the Partridge Family
Every morning we were Laurel and Hardy
If you had a 99.999999 x billion chance to go back in time
And kill Hitler, would you do it?

In other news, gingers have souls
Don't say you know who what when where why has a soul and who what when where why who doesn't?
What?
Gingers have souls, for the last time, gingers do have souls
Shut up Michael, that's just a corporate slave name
Thank you good girl, what's been good duh?
Ever tried hugging a hoodie in the hood yeah?
Remember that guy who said he would kill the prime minister on the morning news?
He was arrested and sent to jail too? I was like, wow, phew
That could have been me, practically just sit here writing here all day
About blowing up the government for fun
The first rule is, "Shut up, there are no rules."
Don't you ever have an original thought for yourself?
Or do you just bow down to anyone willing to demand authority
So let's see, coronavirus wiped out that thing called intelligence
The lockdowns made up for it though
Imagine all the, "Shut up, my grandma just died."
And besides, I never liked the song
I liked Jealous Guy and the other one
Well, well, well, what do we have here now?
A little ragamuffin it appears
You don't know me, you will never know me
But why so serious?
What doesn't kill you makes stranger man
I seen it in a film ages ago man, it was philosophical moment

Yes, so I think for my mental health, music has been the best thing to experience. I can't live without it. Working out also gave me a good foundation to improve myself, and education gave me a lot of confidence back. When I look back on the hallucinations, I imagine if they were to return, what that would be like. Would it take over my life again? Would the hospital come looking for me again? Most of all, though, I look back on the messages an anonymous person sent me from time to time, and I simply wonder who they were and if they are still out there. It can be a crazy world sometimes, and for me, life always got so crazy. In the end, though, I had this creative process with my writing, and I think my mental health condition is part of that, so it's not all negative.

I think in many ways, life on Earth is like a dream, but a collective one, with the laws of physics to govern us and prevent us from floating off to the moon. We are all dreamers in such a vivid world. I think a good person should look to build up their brother, giving one another confidence and encouragement in this life. The mental health system isn't perfect; often, in the hospital, you are being dealt with by people who don't really know you. Once you get out, though, it's back to real life and the community, and the team tends to be a little kinder and more understanding. So we all pull together, try to make something of this life, and hopefully give a lot back to society.

Maybe at times in this memoir, I don't always get it a hundred percent right, like when philosophizing about the hallucinations. However, I wanted to show what the process was actually like for me. This wasn't meant to be an academic book, after all. They have their place, but sometimes a book written from the heart is what we seek. I hope in due time more people like myself come forward with true stories about mental health, then our understanding of these conditions can improve, stigma can be reduced, and overall awareness can become thought-provoking for us all.

In the end, I feel I got better at making rhymes through embracing my idea about the Kal Klein Conspiracy.

THE KAL KLEIN CONSPIRACY

So listen up, I have a question for you
You ever had the pleasure of being treated psychiatrically?
I definitely have, I have been committed hundreds of times practically
Psychiatric injections to serve a correction with my mental abjection
A complete life of utter rejection
More crazy than the invention of parallels dimensions
Fuck redemption, tensions like wounds tear open
Fears flare off causing paranoia, just stay calm and calculated as usual
Lying low as always, never giving a shit, and the conspiracy theories are crucial
The descent into madness is gradual, the hallucinations are grandiose and delusional
Cut my heart out and hand it to you
My soul has been executed
However my heart cannot be executed
I am a poet in disguise
You probably think I am a rapper in disguise
What do you reckon?
I say to my alter ego…
Since I was a kid I had a split personality and I have delusions about living in virtual reality
Imaginary friend that grew into a monster
Wasn't ya?
Let's go back to 99"
When I invented The Kalvin Klein Conspiracy
Just a kid
A five year old with a pen and some paper
A mind sicker than a decapitated gladiator
And I wrote
Antichrist Stomach, Imaginary Knife and Bladeface
I was sick in the head, damn it
In a way I still think that I am
Then the hallucinations
They resurface and bam
The Kal Klein Conspiracy in hallucinations
Kal Klein becomes seemingly real, damn
Because as grown up I only use my right hand
But sometimes I find a message from myself in another hand
Because when I was five I used to always right with my left hand
And I don't know which one is the real me anymore

In a way
It would be this other me
The left handed guy
Technically we are the same person
Story of my life
Only he is like me a but a different version

Antipsychotics for my neurological disorder
Psychiatric narcotics on constant order
As I try to ward off
Constant hallucinations but my shoulders stand broader
'Cause when I was younger, I was smaller and a lot shorter
But as I grew up, I built up and got hell a lot bigger and stronger
Since I was little I've messed in the head
I wasn't always acting like the sharpest tool in the shed
Aliens are better in bed because they have big heads
That's what the hallucinations were saying, that's what they said
They said something about conspiracy, that's what they said
Who would have thought it?
Cause I'm hedging all bets on The Kal Klein Conspiracy
This is all in the past, 1995 is the past, this is all history
Pandemics are getting worse
Animals will rule the world
Humans go underground to survive
This is not a hoax, Goddamnit this is not a lie
Understand? Do you comply?
The reason this is written in the form of a rhyme
Is because I was that guy who wrote the story in 99"
This is not a joke
I have a dissociative fugue state that can emerge in times of crisis
I don't how this is even possible but I swear my life on this
Who would have thought it?
Life is what you make it

MEET KAL KLEIN

Hello
I am your inner conscious known as Kal Klein
Picture this: the depths of your heart so take my name in your hand like a molten sign

Volcano's erupting within the mind spilling over, flowing as wine
The question is what is the conspiracy of Kal Klein?
Realise now that it is like a woven shrine
Read my conspiracy as a science of mind
My heart beats strong, the conspiracy is not wrong
It was a story I made up as a kid that went on for long
What doesn't kill you makes you stronger
All these psychiatric pills build up and fuse over to anger
Damn
Grew up near military hangers out near the association of wranglers
Fell down in the woods one day, woke up as a different person
'Cause I came through a wormhole that I got submersed in
Instantly became a loner, a smoker and a caffeine addict all in one day
Starting reading more and learning about something programmer's call the zen way
I put some coffee in a cup full of sugar and went to school dressed like it was summer in the winter
Gets the blood pumping through the veins
School is out
I'm thirty years old now and my whole life has flashed before my eyes
In that beautiful way, I have already died

There are more of us in The Kal Klein Conspiracy
Meet Philip Matthews and the man who moved invisibly
Meet the woman who never had a name quite interestingly
They were part of the originally story
When Kal Klein acts disorderly
Scarring others in this story you see
That's what the Imaginary Knife was intriguingly
A fingernail sharpened into a blade
Aliens activating time travel from the next age
Find a loophole in the fabric of time
Tear a whole through space and find a page
Exterrestrials will always tamper with television aerials
Causing hallucinations of superpowered immortals
Met one about five years ago
She wore a red dress and said hello
Let's say her name was Lo
But to me she will always be the bike messenger, through the silent bonding of telepathy they seek to avenge her
She was an alien and she played her hand in time travel

Whoever she was...
Some say she was an elegant computer hacker

My book is dangerous
In the wrong hands it will play with ya
Give this memoir to an outcast and he will only get stranger
I need help, I have deep-rooted psychological problems
With beet rooted cheeks and diabolical symptoms
Leading to these phantom outcomes with random rhythms
If it was up to me
I would be locked inside a padded cell
But it's not up to me
Therefore I am free seemingly
I would be a sycamore if I was a tree in Galilee
Always smoking like Tyler Durden
What's this world we are in? Never been a viler vermin
Sometimes as a youngster I would starve myself
Hallucinate from the pure sensation
Lie in bed with a huge ass migraine
And an eagle in my head trying to claw it's way in
I'm still here
Also, I have less empathy and fear
Someone told me, I was biologically engineered

DEAR GOD

God, I pray to you but sometimes I feel like you still ain't listening
But sometimes I remember you used to talk back like you were whispering
Then I think it's just my unconscious mind and I'm doubting you even existing
So I guess it doesn't really matter because your influence is there anyway
And people call you by different names and all the opinions get confusing
Nevermind, this seems like a unique opportunity to talk to you like a channelling
So what's up God? Is it true people get you and the devil mixed up all the time?
And you created the world and the heavens by committing divine suicide?
You caused a plague over Egypt and every first born male to be killed in infanticide?
So you waged war against nations in the olds day causing horrendous genocides
It's all written in your good book, I have one right here next to my bed by the side

Don't you realise through everything that has happened in my life I am dying inside?
All my life I have been trying to hide
As a kid I talked to you by the fireside
I imagined you as a woman in disguise
Maybe you are just a phantom of mind
From your secret admirer, truly yours, Kal Klein

Hello God, I wonder if you even give a damn, it's just I'm kind of mad
Been wondering about that thing you call a divine fucking plan
Maybe I just wasn't part of that procedure
Instead maybe I was just possessed by that thing called legion
That's genesis man, more powerful than God
Like I was sent here to overthrow you
But God is secretly a woman
I saw it in a hallucination about The Kal Klein Conspiracy
It was a banned epistle from some guy called Peter, he spoke to me directly
He always referred to Jesus as she or her, and he gave me a mission
His order was for me to infiltrate the witches order on Earth
It was a female dictatorship that was being described
But God I don't hear your voice no more
In a way, we have a lot in common
We are both powerful beyond measure
Most of the time, we stay out of conflict
I don't relate to much through words in a book
In my own mind and heart I just take a look
Cause I remember you
And we were friends and that's true
You stood up for me and I pulled through
I torture myself with dangerous thoughts
I just won't learn and I cannot be taught
You've left this world behind and it's like you have given up
Most people don't believe you were a girl
I need your help though because I'm struggling again
No one will understand that this is dead serious
You have to listen to me God, I don't want to die like this in vain
Your old friend, Kal Klein
And by the way, do you want to get coffee sometime?

Hello, did you know, envy is a kind of strife?
God ruined my life, and deadly sins are my wife

Cause I've been calling out to you for a long time
I know you are listening God
So let this little light of mine just shine
These aren't just words no more, this is a piece of heaven
So God, how is it down under? Blossoming I hope
You remember that film about the guy who was really manipulative?
It was called Cruel Intentions and was based on Dangerous Liaisons
But at the end he chucked himself in front of a car to save his girlfriend
This is exactly the same thing
I just want you to know I would happily walk through open traffic for you
Most of all in this talk I would never lie to you
Cause at the end of the day you are just another coo
But God, I think I'm special, like no one else
And late at night it's you who I dream about
I can hear your voice sometimes screaming out
Some kind of vulture
Who sometimes sounds like they are trying to shout
So when you yell
I will know you and there will be no doubt
As my own voice is becoming monstrous now
You know that I'm in pain
With this mental illness
And you are driving me insane
So listen up God, I'm going to find you somehow
I'll track you down like you are a missing person, private investigator
Collect clues, gather facts and draw conclusions
Cause this is my memento that I know you can hear
There is no time left, I'm dead, gone with the wind
Damn, fuck you God, all I wanted was to be friends

Psst, listen up, Kal Klein, I have heard that you have died at least inside
I am the one you have missed all the time but I see that you at least have tried
So don't worry, I'm here, there is no indignation nor need to hide
No fear, no doubt, no disbelief or allegories about mystic suicide
No need for mysteries and old stories
I remember you at the fireplace, when you were just a kid
I was listening all along, don't think I wasn't 'cause you were just a kid
I watched over you whilst you lay asleep sound and safe in bed
Realise I am always here but at the same time I don't mean to be inside your head
There is fire inside your heart Kal, you need to channel that energy

Don't waste your life caring too about wealth and having plenty
Even if I was a woman in form and nature I wouldn't tell you
Because if it's supposed to be a secret then what the hell dude?
This is just your imagination at work, what do you think, do you need proof?
What I tell you in secret should be said from the roof
So if you supposing a woman to be truth, then just understand in due time
Everything will make sense, seek after wisdom and look out for the sign
It will not come in the sky, nor by the rain of the night, so hear me, Kal Klein
Why do you love me?
If I was poor would you hug me? Or would you just barge by and shove me?
Just keeping on taking the medication
Trust me it will help in the sense of a spiritual meditation
I will deliver you from all temptations
I am the one you spoke to in grit
I'm calling you to be a warrior
I once husked my voice and fought in a great war
But if you look closely you will see
This is all in your head

The truth is, I'm not a rapper, though. I love the music, the beats, and the lyrical flows. It's just that when you listen so much, you end up trying to create your own rhythms. It's always inevitable. The thing is, I'm a writer, and so far, it has been like writing a book about someone aspiring to be a rapper, but I could never see that far at first. All I could see were the hallucinations for a while. I got better, I survived, and tried my best to thrive and optimize.

Peace to all those who read this book. May your days be filled with love, joy, and happiness.

All I'm saying in this memoir is that if we did live in a Matrix-like simulation, all those hallucinations would be artificially produced. Seeing as there is no sure way to know if we are living in one or not, then chances are, we probably are, but there is still no one way to know, and there will probably never be. You never know, it depends on how you view the world.

If there was a way to prove it, it would depend on what you mean by proof. One clever analysis of proof is: Can you show it live to one hundred percent of the world in a scientific lab setting on television? See? What else do you mean by proof?

Obviously, we don't mean mathematical proof, as high-end physics and math understanding will probably always be reserved for the few educational sparks of genius out there.

In my opinion, mathematical proof would be superior proof if it could be understood across the board. Then we dive into a sea of problems, where the idea of the world being a computer simulation is just a rehash of Pythagorean esoteric knowledge about the world being made of numbers and mathematics. Strangely enough, some people believe this in the modern sense of a more complicated update to sacred geometry. This is fascinating because the mathematical universe, compared to the computer simulation, sounds like a more divine-like analysis.

Not only is classical music all mathematical waves, in this case, those hallucinations would be mathematical because, in this worldview, everything is.

At the same time, I think the Matrix simulation is fairly close to the truth, but it is so close to the cigar that a world built on rules in the computer system, in terms of the hero's journey, is exactly the same thing as saying:

A universe built on all mathematical rules.

The Monad means mind, or sometimes it is called the soul. This can be compared to a super-artificial intelligence. The mind is trapped in a prison-like world from realizing its true potential and conquering all odds in front of it. This is explained in Gnostic schools of thought through a different look at Christianity, where an evil demon has trapped the world and masqueraded as God. Although one might think Neo refers to Neoplatonism, a religion that contested with Christianity and was influenced by Gnosticism.

The classic idea is that Neo represents a messiah-type figure, like Buddha or Jesus. I think the comparison to Buddha does not matter too much because what is important is the shift to an Eastern way of thinking. With the comparison to Jesus with The Matrix's Neo, I think that in the Gnostic school, to some, Neo/Jesus would be here to help free others from the prison, but to others, he would be an enemy, someone ultimately there to still trick them about the nature of "the prison."

It's a good way of looking at it. We do live in a real world, and I don't think we need any more messiah types in this life.

What is needed are people who can make real significant change in society. Ultimately, the stories about simulations and Neo serve as a good way of intuitively understanding psychology in terms of parts of ourselves. Neo represents our higher self, but when we come to find this true self, we find it has become corrupt and must be destroyed so the Phoenix can regenerate itself from its own ashes.

So, as the Black Sun rises in the Hiberian Forests of the Fell Lell Wells, I bid you a fine, fair night.